If I Were To Preach

LITURGICAL-HOMILETIC AIDS FOR CYCLE **B**

George Devine studied at the University of San Francisco and Marquette University. In 1964 he joined the faculty of Seton Hall University, where he has been Associate Professor of Religious Studies. He currently is a Scholar in Residence at the University of San Francisco. For more than a decade he has been involved in the liturgical renewal. He is the author of many reviews and articles which have appeared in leading religious and secular publications.

Other books by him include: *Our Living Liturgy*, Chicago: Claretian Publications, 1966. *Why Read the Old Testament?* Chicago: Claretian Publications. 1966. *To Be A Man* (ed.), Englewood Cliffs, N.J.: Prentice-Hall, Inc., 1969. *Theology in Revolution* (ed.), 1970; *New Dimensions in Religious Experience* (ed.), 1971; *Transformation in Christ*, 1972; *That They May Live* (ed.), 1972; *A World More Human, A Church More Christian* (ed.), 1973; *Liturgical Renewal: An Agonizing Reappraisal*, 1973, all at Staten Island, N.Y.: Alba House. *American Catholicism: Where Do We Go from Here?*, Englewood Cliffs, N.J.: Prentice-Hall, Inc. 1975. *If I Were to Preach, Cycles A, B, & C*, Staten Island, N.Y.: Alba House, 1974-75-76.

Acknowledgements

The author should like to thank those whose cooperation made this volume possible, especially his colleagues and students at Seton Hall University, whose reactions and encouragement will always be treasured, and to the University administration, whose granting of a sabbatical leave facilitated completion of the project. Thanks are also due the University of San Francisco, where the author was welcomed as Scholar-in-Residence during said leave, under Dr. Lloyd D. Luckmann and Dean Wm. V. Burgess. The physical appearance of the book is the fine work of the Fathers and Brothers of St. Paul, as part of their publications apostolate. Lastly, the author thanks those closest to him during the book's preparation—his wife Joanne and their children.

If I Were To Preach

LITURGICAL-HOMILETIC AIDS FOR CYCLE **B**

by George Devine
ASSOCIATE PROFESSOR OF RELIGIOUS STUDIES
SETON HALL UNIVERSITY

ALBA · HOUSE NEW · YORK

SOCIETY OF ST. PAUL, 2187 VICTORY BLVD., STATEN ISLAND, NEW YORK 10314

Library of Congress Cataloging in Publication Data

Devine, George, 1941-
Liturgical-homiletic aids for cycle B.

His If I were to preach; v. 2)
1. Church year sermons.
2. Catholic Church—
Sermons. 3. Sermons, American. I. Title.
BX1756.D47.13 vol. 2   252'.02s
[251'.08]   75-15822
ISBN   0-8189-0320-1

Nihil Obstat:
James T. O'Connor, S.T.D.
Censor Librorum

Imprimatur:
+ James P. Mahoney, D.D.
Vicar General, Archdiocese of New York
May 16, 1975

*Designed, printed and bound in the United States of
America by the Fathers and Brothers of the Society of St. Paul,
2187 Victory Boulevard, Staten Island, New York, 10314,
as part of their communications apostolate.*

1 2 3 4 5 6 7 8 9 (Current Printing: first digit).

For my daughter,
Annemarie Victoria

CONTENTS

Foreword		1
1.	First Sunday of Advent	3
2.	Feast of the Immaculate Conception	6
3.	Second Sunday of Advent	9
4.	Third Sunday of Advent	12
5.	Fourth Sunday of Advent	15
6.	Christmas	18
7.	Holy Family	21
8.	Solemnity of Mary, Mother of God	24
9.	Second Sunday after Christmas	27
10.	Epiphany	30
11.	Sunday after January 6	33
12.	First Sunday of Lent	37
13.	Second Sunday of Lent	40
14.	Third Sunday of Lent	43
15.	Fourth Sunday of Lent	46
16.	Fifth Sunday of Lent	49
17.	Palm Sunday	52
18.	Holy Thursday	54
19.	Good Friday	57
20.	Easter Vigil/Easter Sunday	60
21.	Second Sunday of Easter	65
22.	Third Sunday of Easter	68
23.	Fourth Sunday of Easter	71
24.	Fifth Sunday of Easter	74
25.	Sixth Sunday of Easter	77
26.	Seventh Sunday after Easter	80
27.	Ascension	83

28. Pentecost 86
29. Trinity Sunday 89
30. Assumption 92
31. Second Sunday of the Year 95
32. Third Sunday of the Year 98
33. Fourth Sunday of the Year 101
34. Fifth Sunday of the Year 104
35. Sixth Sunday of the Year 107
36. Seventh Sunday of the Year 110
37. Eighth Sunday of the Year 113
38. Ninth Sunday of the Year 116
39. Tenth Sunday of the Year 119
40. Eleventh Sunday of the Year 122
41. Twelfth Sunday of the Year 125
42. Thirteenth Sunday of the Year 128
43. Fourteenth Sunday of the Year 131
44. Fifteenth Sunday of the Year 134
45. Sixteenth Sunday of the Year 137
46. Seventeenth Sunday of the Year 140
47. Eighteenth Sunday of the Year 143
48. Nineteenth Sunday of the Year 146
49. Twentieth Sunday of the Year 149
50. Twenty-First Sunday of the Year 152
51. Twenty-Second Sunday of the Year 155
52. Twenty-Third Sunday of the Year 158
53. Twenty-Fourth Sunday of the Year 161
54. Twenty-Fifth Sunday of the Year 164
55. Twenty-Sixth Sunday of the Year 167
56. Twenty-Seventh Sunday of the Year 170
57. Twenty-Eighth Sunday of the Year 173
58. Twenty-Ninth Sunday of the Year 176
59. Thirtieth Sunday of the Year 179
60. Feast of All Saints 182
61. Thirty-First Sunday of the Year 185
62. Thirty-Second Sunday of the Year 188
63. Thirty-Third Sunday of the Year 191
64. Last Sunday of the Year 194

If I Were To Preach

Foreword

Following the volume authored a year prior (for the "A" cycle of liturgical readings in the Lectionary), this is a series of homiletic suggestions for the Sundays and holy days of obligation in the liturgical year according to the "B" cycle. As in the previous volume, the homiletic materials suggested are from the viewpoint of a contemporary Catholic layman and reflect what I would have uttered in the preaching of the liturgy *If I Were to Preach*.* However, this volume differs from its predecessor in that its analysis of the Biblical themes of the liturgy will attempt more "depth," presuming that the "A" cycle has taken a more "introductory" approach, accompanied in many cases by at least some sort of attempt to connect liturgy and the life that must radiate from it in a Christian community. Towards the continuing establishment and strengthening of just such a connection, this work is offered.

George Devine
Lumberville, Pa.
December 31, 1974

* This is the title of the previous volume (Staten Island, N.Y. Alba House, 1974), and of the final one in this series as well 1976).

An explanatory note:

Unlike its immediate predecessor, this volume of *If I Were to Preach* does not provide suggestions for the various liturgical options proposed by the Church (i.e., penitential rite, eucharistic prayer and acclamation), or for the sung or spoken response of the congregation (hymns, antiphonal recitations, etc.). The previous volume, for Cycle "A", affords numerous examples of how these decisions should be taken in accord with the nature of the feast, the lessons of Scripture on the feast in question, and of course the practical resources of the particular worshipping community. Although there will be obvious differences between the liturgical cycles, there may be some benefit in considering the models in Cycle A from *If I Were to Preach.*

First Sunday of Advent

The first reading (Is 63:16-17, 19; 64:2-7) *is one of those prophetic passages asking God to be present with his people and awaiting his coming; the same theme is expressed in the Response. As in the first reading, the second selection* (1 Cor 1:3-9) *thanks God for his concern for his people, as manifested in the New Covenant in Jesus. The Gospel* (Mk 13:33-37) *reminds Jesus' followers that the coming of the Lord is unpredictable.*

We do not know when

The Gospel passage in today's liturgy reminds us of a familiar facet of Christian revelation: we cannot know when it will be that the Lord will come in glory. The fullness of Jesus' presence will literally be "the end of time," that goal towards which all time is directed, and by which all time, all human history, can derive its ultimate meaning. But we cannot know how much time in human history shall have elapsed when Jesus will be present in his fullness and in the final glory we expect.

One practical application of this Gospel is immediately clear to us in terms of our lives: that end of time, that culmination of history, which we call "the second coming," is literally unpredictable. (This is important to remember, since there have been people throughout history who have claimed to be able to predict with some accuracy the time and manner in which the Lord would come in his final glory.)

We can expect unpredictability

This element of unpredictability is part and parcel of the very end, the very goal, of history in the Christian view: the fullness of presence of Jesus the Risen Lord in the world and in final triumph. So it should not be too surprising that there will be *many* elements of unpredictability *throughout* Christian life, both in the life of the Church, over-all, and in the lives of each and every one of us, individually.

Most of us like to think in terms of our lives as being under control, where everything is "all squared away." Many of us plan our lives in such a way that, after a certain stage, we imagine that everything will simply fall into place, nicely and neatly. Once graduation comes, once the wedding takes place, once the promotion is given or retirement begins, or whatever, we seem to feel, *then* life will work out. Everything else will simply fall into line with the main event on which we have depended so much.

Life is not a movie

Of course, real life seldom works that way. But we don't like to face that fact. Many of us can remember the romantic movies of the 1930s, 1940s and 1950s—they're often shown on the "late show" on television today—where everything works out fine for the long-suffering hero or heroine, once that particular magic moment occurs in the story. All of a sudden, the boy from the poor neighborhood who struggled with obscurity is hitting a home run in Yankee Stadium, or leading a symphony orchestra. Or the little girl from the farm is understudy to the star, and she takes over when the star gets laryngitis, and gets the big chance she's been waiting for all along. And the music swells, and the crowd cheers, and everything is fine from there on in. No, life doesn't work out like that at all. And when we try to escape from that fact or ignore it, that's probably why so many of us get interested in such fantastic movies. Even when something like that *does* actually take place in an individual's life, it's very rare, and we usually like to think that since it happened in one instance, it can happen in our own as well. But it seldom ever does.

Soothsayers are always with us

There have been people throughout Christian history who have tended to seize upon some date in the future and say that it is *then* that Jesus will be present in all his fullness, in final triumph. At one time, people believed it would be in the year of our Lord 1,000—the millennium. Some people, perhaps confused by an exaggeration of private revelations, felt it would be in the year of our Lord 1960. And so on it goes.

There is an end, a goal, to Christian history, in which Jesus will be fully present in a manner unlike that which we now know. But we cannot make it happen by attempting predictions. We cannot know when it is that this fuller presence (or *parousia*) will be. All we can do, all we *need* do, is trust in the Lord and abide in him, realizing that he is with us as we await the *final* victory of Jesus over sin and death for all, as manifest in his coming again in glory.

This means an ongoing hope in the Lord, with reliance on the companion virtues of faith in him and a life of love in his name, so that we make straight the way of the Lord who comes. It means, too, adjusting to all the unpredictable, and perhaps sometimes upsetting, elements in each of our own individual lives with that same faith, that same hope, that same love, so that our lives will truly bear witness to the Christ who has died, is risen and will come again.

Immaculate Conception (December 8)

The first reading (Gn 3:9-15, 20) brings us the Old Testament image of man's initial rejection of divine friendship, to be repaired through the coming of the Savior in a later phase of Salvation-History. It is this Christ whom Paul will praise in his letter to the Church at Ephesus (Ep 1:3-6, 11-12). The receptivity of Mary to the will of God will be a means to the coming of the Messiah, as the Gospel according to Luke stresses (Lk 1:26-38).

At the outset, man rejected God

The story we read today, from the Book of Genesis in the Old Testament, is sadly familiar. The point of this story is to show how man, at the very outset of human history, in some way rejected God's offer of friendship. A breach now existed between man and God, and between man and man—even division of individual men and women within themselves—that could be righted or healed only by God's merciful love. This relationship between man and God, man and fellow man, man and himself, was so damaged at the origins of human life in the world that this sin or alienation is called *original*. We learn from the Scriptures that this sin, this separation of man from God, has minimized man's ability to know and love the Lord, and is symbolized in a variety of painful symptoms, including the very experience of human death.

Man's sorry estrangement from the Deity, and from even

himself, is seen in a history of wars, injustices, hatreds, greeds that make up a woeful list indeed. These things, all too often, make up the headlines of our newspapers or the contents of our radio and television news broadcasts.

If all this is so, we might ask ourselves, what about the repair afforded by the coming of Jesus the Christ? Is there not *at-one-ment*, is there not a new order of salvation, since the Word became flesh and dwelt among us? After all, it is this saving incarnation of the Son of God which Paul praises, so enthusiastically, in today's reading from the Letter to the Ephesians, and which we celebrate in this Eucharist, for the feast of the Immaculate Conception of Jesus' mother, the virgin Mary.

Man can still reject grace

Here, we must remember that the saving grace of Jesus, the Son of God sent to bring men and women back to the Father, is not received, nor accepted universally. God's grace does not save those who refuse it, or who are unable to receive it owing to ignorance, bigotry or some other circumstance.

Signs of estrangement

So, until the Lord comes in final glory, we may expect to see the signs of a humanity estranged from its Creator and even from itself. But with this there comes a call and a challenge, for each of us as members of Christ's body in the world, his Church, to bring God's saving grace and ourselves and our fellow human beings closer and closer together, as a means to that coming in the glory of the Savior.

We will be called upon to do this, each of us in his or her own way, in the face of the very discouraging circumstances we have just made mention of: wars, famine, strife, injustice, alienation. We will be called to respond, as did Mary, to the will of God in hope and faith, "...for nothing is impossible with God." For this "...God chose us in (Christ) before the world began, to be holy and blameless in his sight, to be full of love...." In the same way God chose Mary, whom we celebrate today and imitate every day, and who answered as each of us must, in hopeful and creative response to the will and the Word of God, that Christ's grace may permeate the world.

Second Sunday of Advent

The first reading (Is 40:1-5, 9-11) and the Gospel (Mk 1:1-8) both utter the cry to men that they must make straight and prepare the way of the Lord who comes. In the second reading (2 P 3:8-14) two lessons are conveyed: one is that the day of the Lord's coming cannot be hastened (an important notion for the early Christians, who anxiously awaited it); the second is that earthly things will be obsolete in the Lord's final coming in glory.

Preparation, if not prediction

In last week's liturgy we saw that the coming of the Lord in final glory cannot be predicted, but it can be prepared for. We can, as the prophet says, "make straight the way of the Lord!" And we should consider some of the implications of this for our lives.

We have considered, before, the connected virtues of faith, hope and love in the Christian life, and we would do well to spell out these considerations even further. When we abide in the hope that the Lord will come again in glory, we act accordingly—we live lives of Christian love.

Make ready the way

The way the prophet expresses it, "Make ready the way of the Lord, clear him a straight path," should make it evident, in a symbolic way, that we must remove any obstacle to the Lord's coming and abiding with us. Sacramental theologians have long told us that man cannot limit the power of God to be present in his Church, but that men *can* refuse to allow the grace of God to take effect in their own individual lives.* The same applies in our present frame of reference: by our own hardness of heart, we can make ourselves—and others around us, too—less receptive to the Lord who is to come. We can render ourselves—and others also—resistant to the grace of God that is offered to us in the person of Jesus.

Time to take stock

Advent is traditionally a time of taking stock of ourselves and our lives, in preparation for the celebration of Christmas. And it is a good time, too, to take stock of ways in which we might be resisting the presence of Jesus in our lives and in the lives of others we know in the world around us.

The second reading, from a pastoral letter of our first Holy Father, Peter, tells us that the things we put so much stock in here on earth will be destroyed anyway; they are not of lasting value, ultimately. There are two possible conclusions we can draw from this. One, which many have tended to hold, is that since nothing in this life is important anyway, there is no reason to take it seriously. This type of attitude, for too long and among too many people, has led to a lack of sufficient Christian interest in some very real problems in the world. But the second possible conclusion is that since all we know on earth will fail to endure, and cannot be held onto by us, we must use all of it as best we can in witnessing to and praising the Creator of all of it and all of us, in making straight the way of the Lord.

In this connection, let us ask ourselves: has my attitude towards the goods of this world helped to make me and others around me more receptive to the coming of the Lord? Or has

* This is expressed in the traditional notion *obex*, or obstacle to grace.

my attitude towards worldly goods stood in the way? Have my selfishness, my clutching, my hoarding prevented me from opening my heart to the grace of God and to my fellow creatures? Or have I viewed all things in life as gifts from God, to be used unselfishly so as to praise him and make myself and others more readily open to his grace?

Legitimate concern or preoccupied materialism?

Often we hear people talk about the things they want, and the things they have worked for, with a certain amount of determination and pride. To a certain point, this is both understandable and legitimate. Each of us needs certain things for our lives. But some people speak of these things with a passion and almost a panic, which is really unreasonable. And when such people fail to recognize that the goods of this life are not *really* theirs in the first place, they stand as obstacles in the way of the Lord's coming into their hearts. Moreover, they might be perpetuating some of the social injustices that make it difficult for the Lord to come into the hearts of men in general.

Not only during this Christmas season now approaching, but at all times, let us celebrate the coming of the Lord into history to save men, by acknowledgement of his lordship over all things, and our willingness to share with those who are in need and who are less fortunate than we may be. There are numerous opportunities to do this, not only in one particular instance or another, but most importantly by a state of mind dedicated to the leveling of inequities, and the making-straight of the way of the Lord.

Third Sunday of Advent

The first reading (Is 61:1-2, 10-11) foreshadows the coming of the kingdom, a recurrent theme in prophetic literature and in the Advent liturgy. The second reading (1 Thes 5:16-24) provides instructions for Christians who wait for the fuller coming in the final presence of Christ the King. The Gospel (Jn 1:6-8, 19-28) reiterates the prophet's command to make the way of the Lord ready, and focuses our attention on the coming of Jesus into public life.

During this Advent season, in light of the Biblical readings of the liturgy, we are particularly concerned with the ways in which we might prepare the way of the Lord, and help make ourselves and our world more receptive to his coming in glory, and his coming into the lives and the hearts of each and every one of us.

Good advice

With this concern in mind we have heeded the words of the Epistles of the New Testament these past weeks, dwelling on the advice the Apostles, the first Bishops, gave to the earliest Christians as they waited in hope for the coming of our Lord Jesus Christ. We have heard how the early Christians, and ourselves, have been warned against clutching too tightly the goods of this world and this life, and how we have been told that we should share these with fellow creatures in praise of the Creator of us all. Now, we have another lesson from the Epistles of the New Testament, and it is very consistent with the lessons we have learned up until now, even though it is perhaps more simple.

Rejoice always. The instruction seems almost *too* simple. After all, is there not much more to life's ups and downs than simply rejoicing? But we are told, plainly and tersely, to rejoice always. We are told further: do not stifle the spirit. What do these words mean for us?

Rejoicing and celebration

To rejoice in the spirit is to celebrate. And to celebrate is to take full measure of what we have and who we are, and to proclaim it as fully as we can. And what we are is the People of God, chosen by him in covenant and saved in the death and resurrection of Jesus.

This means that even in the time of waiting which we call Advent, we are keenly aware that the Lord is with us, in the Church and in the sacramental presence of Jesus, most especially in the Holy Eucharist. For this reason, even in the middle of a so-called penitential season, we are called upon to rejoice.

Rejoice even in disappointment

And even in the disappointing days of life which are all too frequent and familiar for each and every one of us, we are called upon to rejoice ... to take stock of the good things that God has done for us and to be glad for them, even in the face of whatever may frustrate or depress us for a time. This is hard to say, and even harder to do, when we survey some of the gloomy landscapes of life's failures.

But the Christian can rejoice always because the *important* thing in life—nothing less than everlasting life itself—is won in the death and resurrection of Jesus, who comes again. This is why the Christian can always find something to be glad about, and this is why, whenever Christians get together to worship, we say that this action is a *celebration*.

But this attitude of celebration does not apply only to our formal worship or liturgy. It is an attitude which should permeate the life of a Christian all the time and everywhere.

The "special ordinary"

Some years ago, a well-known Catholic artist and author, Sister Corita Kent, made mention of what she called "the special ordinary" as a component of Christian life. The idea behind this expression was that, since we are part of a creation and a life redeemed by the risen Lord, everything in that creation and everything in that life must be special. As a result, we should take special notice of everything in our lives, however ordinary it may seem to us at the time, for it is truly a special indication of God's love and abiding presence in our lives.

Our daily associations with friends or co-workers, our getting dressed in the morning, our meals, our activities from day to day, however humble these may be, and whatever unpleasant elements may intrude themselves upon these daily aspects of life, such activities and elements are occasions for us to celebrate, and to rejoice in who we are as members of the chosen and redeemed people of God. And through us, all men might believe, since our very lives of celebration will bear witness to the light which is Christ.

Fourth Sunday of Advent

The first reading (2 S 7:1-5, 8-11, 16) and the Gospel (Lk 1: 26-38) both allude to the Davidic kingship, which in the New Testament is fulfilled in Jesus. A key element here is continuity, a facet stressed in the first reading in the Old Testament. The second reading's (Rm 16:25-27) emphasis is on continuity also, and upon man's reasons to praise the God who constantly abides with him.

Seeing through things

Bishop Fulton J. Sheen, in his TV series "Life Is Worth Living" in the 1950s, often liked to give definitions which would stick in the minds of his listeners, and which would have some basis in philosophy, etymology and some of the other studies on which this noted author and lecturer would touch. In one of his talks, Bishop Sheen described humor as the ability to see through things. And, of course, the implication was that the Lord must have a good sense of humor. Fifteen years later, in the transition from the 1960s to the 1970s, a well-known Protestant theologian, Robert E. Neale, brought out the same notion, in his book entitled *In Praise of Play*. The thrust of Neale's reasoning is that if God can see through everything, he must therefore have the best sense of humor of all! If we want an example of this, we hardly have to look any further than today's first reading, from the second book of Samuel in the

Old Testament, to see the divine sense of humor at work.

In this passage from Scripture, we see King David concerned about the fact that his own dwelling-place is rather luxurious by the standards of his time and circumstances; it is made of cedar. But the sacred ark of God is housed in a tent. David begins to feel that perhaps he should do better for the Lord than that. And what does the Lord answer him through Nathan? To paraphrase:

God does not need man

"If I, as Lord and God, am capable of taking care of the people of Israel throughout the ages, and leading the Chosen People to the Promised Land over all the Egyptians and Amalekites and Canaanites and other enemies, do I *really* need the likes of *you* to find me a place to live? This is like the president of a large bank asking somebody if he can spare a dime!" This crude paraphrase, like the Biblical passage from which it is taken, should point out that God needs man for nothing. God is self-sufficient. God is never in need of help from man, but always ready to *be* of help to man. Man never needs to wonder what he can do *for* God, since there is nothing man can do for God. All man needs to be concerned with is how he can best respond to what God does for *him*.

Even then, so far as the matter of worship is concerned, this passage from Scripture seems to make clear—as do a number of other Biblical texts—that God is not concerned with elaborate forms of surroundings for worship. Once more, we see a picture of a God who would *serve*, and not *be* served. The type of dwelling which man provides for the sacred ark hardly seems to concern God in this story. And in other passages throughout the Old Testament, we see the prophets chiding Israel because they—and not the God they propose to honor—will be seen as putting too much stress on the physical surroundings and attributes of the Temple. The prophets repeatedly tell Israel that their keeping of the Law is far more important than the beauty of the Temple, which *men* seem to need far more than God does.

Unrealistic standards

At this particular time of year, just as Christmas approaches, some of us tend to measure ourselves against some rather unrealistic goals. We may compare ourselves with others, unfavorably, in terms of what we will have to wear at Christmas, or what we will have for our Christmas dinner, or in what sort of place our holiday celebration will be. And we may look at our own church, and compare it to some others, and think that we are coming off rather poorly in the comparison. If only we could do better, we might say to ourselves.

God might laugh at us

And God, who has a sense of humor—*the* sense of humor—might laugh at this, although lovingly, since the things that preoccupy us are not all that important. The gifts we offer to God, and to one another, at Christmas and at all other times, are important insofar as they are expressions of love, and whether or not they are elaborate doesn't matter in the least. What *does* matter is that we love God and in his name love one another, and allow his saving grace to enter and change our lives and the lives of those around us. This is not something we can do for God, but something we can allow God to do in and for us. And that is all he asks.

Christmas

The first reading for the Vigil Mass promises vindication in the Lord (Is 62:1-5). The promise is fulfilled, Paul proclaims, in Jesus (Ac 13:16-17; 22-25), who is Emmanuel, or the sign of God's being with his People (Mt 1:1-25).

The Mass at Midnight, similarly, shows the coming of a great light (Is 9:1-6), in a portion of the same book attributed to Isaiah, but of earlier authorship from a different source ("first Isaiah"). This is the manifestation of God's grace in glory, Paul writes to Titus (Tt 2:11-4), as will be celebrated in the angel's hymn, in the Gospel according to Luke (2:1-14).

The coming of the savior is reward for the faithful, in the first reading of the Mass at Dawn (Is 62:11-12), the personification of the kindness and love of God (Tt 3:4-7), adored by humanity as represented by the shepherds in the Gospel narrative of Luke (Lk 2:15-20).

The savior who comes will announce peace and good news, in the initial passage of the Mass During the Day (Is 52:7-10). Prior to the New Covenant, the coming of this savior was not always clear, but it is in Jesus (Heb 1:1-6), the perfection and personification of God's communication with his People (Jn 1:1-18).

Christmas anticipation

Many of us can remember Christmas, in childhood, as a

time of great anticipation. And those among us who are *still* in childhood will readily know the feeling of excitement that comes weeks and weeks before Christmas, when the first decorations and signs go up around the shopping districts, and when the first displays of toys and gifts appear. There is a special thrill, each year, when a child calculates the number of weeks— then days—remaining until Christmas actually comes at last. The most exciting day, probably, is Christmas Eve, when all the images of Santa Claus and his reindeer enter the head of a child—and many an adult, too—bringing with them the expectation of gifts and joy beyond imagining. The tree, the tinsel, the carols, all come together for a glorious climax as the 24th of December turns into the 25th.

Christmas morning

Christmas morning, is there a child anywhere who sleeps late? The living-room beckons, with its presents from the delivery of the previous night. And, one by one, they are opened with excitement and glee, the wrapping-papers strewn about in a frenzy of delight. Finally, there comes a moment when it must be realized that there are no more packages to open. The collection of gifts, for which a child's heart has prepared for weeks and weeks, is suddenly concluded. Next, there will be another phase, though: the initial enjoyment and exhibition of the new treasures, each one still in perfect, brand-new condition, ready to show off to one and all.

But, for a child, the day winds down quickly. There are, indeed, no more gaily-wrapped packages to explore, and the once-sparkling-new gifts are old—hours old! Almost a whole *day* old! It becomes time, soon enough, for new clothes to be put away into chests-of-drawers, and new toys to be put in their places. Soon enough, all too soon, one of the beautiful new gifts—a doll, a toy car or truck, a drum—falls prey to an accident of hard use, and is broken. It may not be long before another follows suit.

And Christmas, before the day of December 25th is spent,

is often a bit of a let-down for a child. The anticipation, almost always, is so much greater than the reality.

We are all children

What has just been described is perhaps normal or typical for children. When we mature, of course, we have different kinds of expectations. But even then, it so often happens, what we look forward to is greater than what actually takes place, since our real experience can hardly live up to our imaginations. In this regard, every one of us is a little bit like the child at Christmas.

But the Lord, in the central meaning of the Christmas event, turns the tables on us, so to speak. He provides us with a reality far greater than its anticipation. As we see in the Scriptures for the Christmas Mass, the people of Israel had long waited for a savior, and in many ways imagined who he would be, what he would be like, what he would do for them. In the main, it was expected that he would be a great teacher, possibly someone, too, who would be an effective leader for Israel as both a civil and religious nation, likely involved in some sort of political activism.

The reality exceeds anticipation

What God provides, of course, is far beyond that sort of anticipation: his own Son, the second Person of the Blessed Trinity, the Word of God—the Lord's communication to the People of God—made flesh. The prophetic literature of the Old Testament could only provide a hint of what was really to come in the person of Jesus, the Messiah who would transcend the expectations of all men. He would give not political leadership, not mere human charism, but the very Bread of Life, which we celebrate in the Christmas Mass and in every Mass.

We express thanks for a gift, at Christmas and all other times, by partaking of it. Let us do this with the gift of Jesus in the Holy Eucharist . . . at Christmas and in every Mass.

Sunday in the Octave of Christmas (Holy Family)

The first reading from the Old Testament comes from the sapiential book of Sirach, recommended to us as a model for mutual respect in a household (Si 3:2-6, 12-14). The sorts of virtues required in all human living, particularly family life, are described in our second reading, from Paul's pastoral letter to the Colossians (Col 3:12-21). In the reading from the Gospel according to Luke (Lk 2:22-40), we see exemplified the importance of observing religious law in the life of a family, and in particular for children.

A model in Jesus

We see from the story given us in today's Gospel, according to Luke, that Mary and Joseph quickly and fully conformed to what the law of their religious society expected of them, especially with regard to the child Jesus. This was not insignificant in the boy's life, as the evangelist implies: "When they had fulfilled all the prescriptions of the law of the Lord, they returned to Galilee and their own town of Nazareth. The child grew in size and strength, filled with wisdom, and the grace of God was upon him."

Throughout Christian tradition, we have seen the Church emphasize the keeping of religious obligations not only for the sake of those adults who observe them, but in a special way for the religious education of younger members of the community of faith. Generally, members of the Church have supported this point of view, and have found themselves able to carry it out without great difficulty.

Resistance to authority

But in recent times, things have become different. These have been times, our commentators and observers have reminded us, in which young people tend to resent or resist the heavy hand of authority, and in which one generation will not see things as another age group does.

In family after family, there are children or teenagers who seem to reject the codes of religious observance which their elders hold sacred. This sort of situation can be problematic and perplexing for a conscientious parent.

Lessons to remember

Perhaps the first thing which should be remembered is that a young person will tend to internalize the religious values of elders, if not all along throughout life, then certainly at one time or another in the maturing process. This means that, even after a time of adolescent rebellion, a grown person tends to consider most seriously those elements which were communicated to him or her as a youngster, and to see their value. Realization of this fact implies two further lessons:

First, it cannot be emphasized strongly enough that regular religious observance has little chance of flourishing among children of those who do not take such observance seriously themselves. We are all familiar with the stereotype of the parent who imposes religious observance upon his or her children but does not practice accordingly. Such a parent speaks more dramatically by example than by words, and the more dramatic statement—the example—has a good chance of making its mark long after the words have lost their force. In a household where church is a place not to go, or participation in the liturgy is considered unimportant, regardless of what formal statements are made to the contrary, it is not terribly likely that young people will grow in a love of religion.

On the other hand, we are taught a second lesson: adolescents *do* tend to rebel against various forms of authority and conformity. This realization does *not* constitute an argument for laxity in matters of religion. But we should examine the total picture of the authority images in a household. Do parents (and other surrounding figures) make more demands than are really necessary, at one time? If so, they may present a child or an adolescent with such an unbearable burden that he or she will rebel indiscriminately, even irrationally, rejecting the important things along with, or even instead of, the ones which are not all that important. Some parents—and other authority figures, like teachers—present an image of authority which is excessive and unreasonable; in so doing they *invite* rebellion, on a grand scale.

Jesus loved and understood

Finally, we should consider the fact that Jesus, while firm, was loving and understanding. Those of us who may be dismayed because our children, or other young people in our charge, appear not to observe religious obligations should never cease to love and understand them and—most importantly— to *show* our love, kindly and tenderly. It is by doing this, all the while maintaining our own religious observance, that we show them the Christ whom we are drawn to, and would have *them* drawn to, in lives of worship.

Octave of Christmas: Solemnity of Mary, Mother of God (January 1)

The first reading from the Old Testament book of Numbers (Nb 6:22-27) opens with a blessing appropriate for the new year, and reflective of the abiding faith of Israel in Yahweh, their Lord. The transition of God's plan for salvation from Old to New Covenant is effective in part through Mary, as Paul points out in the second reading (Gal 4:4-7). In the selection from the Gospel according to Luke (Lk 2:16-21), we are shown Jesus as the fulfillment of the expectations of Israel.

The Biblical readings for the liturgy of this day reflect several themes which are intermingled in the lessons of the Holy Scriptures, chosen for our meditation by the Church at the start of a new year. One of these, surely, is our sharing in divine sonship with Jesus, who causes us to enter into a new relationship with God the Father. Another, of course, is the special role of the Virgin Mary, which in itself indicates new dignity for humankind in general and womankind in particular.

Some people have been led to wonder, recently, if these themes might not be somewhat contradictory. Is it possible to speak of the full dignity of woman in God's plan for salvation if we continue to speak of God in masculine terms, as "Father"?

Human language fails

We should remember from the outset that all human language, in attempting to describe the Divine Persons, will necessarily fall short. Even our best efforts will fail. The greater theologians of our Christian history recognized this at once. And those theologians who were not so great—who might have thought they could somehow "define" God—soon learned of the limitations of human knowledge in the face of divine mystery. The best we can do, in trying to speak of the deity, is describe our relationship to God as revealed. The best we can offer is not definition, which is limiting and perhaps final, but rather *description*. This was attempted by the People of God, led by the Spirit, in the formation of the religious literature of first the Old Testament and then the New.

There are many images which come to us from Holy Scripture, by way of attempting to show how God relates to us and how we should relate to God. In some places, God is a shepherd, in others a judge; in still others, God is like a bridegroom. Jesus, in the New Testament, is likened to a lamb, to a temple, and to a king. All of these things are *images*, ways of helping us comprehend God, but not *definitions* of God as such.

Images are not literal

So far as we know, Jesus was not a tender of sheep in the literal sense. Certainly, he was not a temple in the sense of a physical building, nor a lamb. The community of Jesus is described as a kingdom, but not of this world as we know it, so the image of Jesus as a king will necessarily miss the mark. Since Jesus, the Second Person of the Trinity, actually did take on human flesh, he is easier to envision or identify with than the other Persons of the Godhead, who are described in even more difficult human images. Is God, the First Person of the Trinity, actually to be pictured in judge's robes, or holding a shepherd's crook? Did God actually marry, as did the prophet Hosea who supplies the image of God as bridegroom and Israel as bride? And can the Holy Spirit be summed up simply as a wind, as in Genesis, or as the fluttering dove we think of so often?

These images of the Bible, taken quite literally, can be misleading. So it is when we speak of God the Father. We cannot really attribute to the First Person of the Trinity a sex, masculine or feminine. But, since fatherhood has been identified over the centuries with protection and providence and love, we tend to describe our loving and provident God as Father. This image, as used in Paul's letter to the Galatians today, can be a beautiful one and a helpful one in understanding our relationship to God.

At the same time, it is only right to note that over the centuries we have not appreciated enough the role of woman and her dignity. Until very recently, even the physical contribution of the mother to a new life was not understood adequately by the life sciences. We have tended to perpetuate a host of mistakes and cliches about woman in society generally, in the family, and in various institutions.

Mary's image is helpful

In the face of what is obviously ignorance or prejudice concerning women, the image of Mary as proposed to us by the Church can be helpful in many ways. Many of our religious writers and leaders, including even the Holy Father, have suggested this. Of course, Mary is, like Jesus, an actual historical person, who played a real role in history. Mary is, like Jesus, somewhat easy to identify with. Mary is precursor and model for generations of Christians, male and female, married and celibate, young and old, throughout the centuries of the history of the People of God.

The person of Mary as presented to us in the New Testament writings, and as understood in the developing tradition of the Church, is creative and caring, and a witness to the will of God. And those who think Mary to be only passive have misread the courage she necessarily exhibited in her early participation in a movement which challenged the "Establishment" of Judaism in her time.

When we call God, as Paul suggests today, "Abba!" or "Father!" we mean and do no disservice to the dignity of woman in Salvation-History. At the same time, we can only celebrate that dignity if we adequately celebrate Mary.

Second Sunday after Christmas

The Old Testament reading from the Book of Sirach, in the wisdom literature collection, is an example of the literary device of personification typical of this body of literature, especially with regard to the very figure of wisdom itself. Wisdom as faith is implied by Paul in his letter to the Ephesians, lauding their "innermost vision." The Gospel selection is the famous "logos prologue" to the Gospel according to John.

There is no pursuit more important, today's Scriptures tell us, than the cultivation of wisdom. This does not mean simply human knowledge, or what we today might think of as "technology." But the reference is to wisdom of the highest sort: *divine* wisdom. Knowledge of the Almighty is above all other goods in the scheme of things.

We cannot comprehend God

Needless to say, those of us who seek knowledge of the deity will necessarily be disappointed and frustrated by even our own best efforts. God is, ultimately, beyond human comprehension. Obviously, only limited apprehension of the divine is available to even the most learned and insightful people.

The Jews of the Old Testament period who found themselves in Covenant with God surely understood this as they developed the rich wisdom literature from which we read today. So did Paul the Apostle as he communicated the good news of the New Covenant to the early Christian community at Ephesus in Asia Minor.

Each must attempt to understand

However, each of us is obliged to come to an understanding of the Persons of the Trinity to whatever extent we can. This does not mean that each of us should presume that we will become parties to a special sort of knowledge (although some early Christians called "gnostics" erroneously got this notion). Nor does it mean we should all become professional theologians or philosophers. It does mean that each of us, depending on his or her circumstances and opportunities, should take account of and show regard for the wisdom that is present in our midst in the person of Jesus, the Word of God made flesh and dwelling among us.

There are various ways in which we will have opportunities to encounter this supreme good of divine wisdom in the community of Jesus which is his Church.

We meet divine wisdom in liturgy

One way will be, of course, the liturgy itself. Each time the liturgy is celebrated, we meet the Word of God in Sacred Scripture. The texts can often "speak for themselves" eloquently, rich with Biblical imagery. As our first reading today tells us, "Wisdom sings her own praises." However, it is often the case that one or another of the Biblical expressions needs some explanation or application by one of the more learned members of our community. This is why a priest or deacon gives a homily, to make clear the meanings of the Scriptural selections of the liturgy for our own everyday lives. (For the same reason, a commentator or lector at Mass often gives a brief remark illuminating the themes of the readings.)

The Church offers opportunities

Another way is participation in whatever opportunities the

Church locally affords us for our own continuing education. Sometimes there will be a special program in our own parish or diocese, or a neighboring one, which we can take part in. This is frequently the case during the Lenten season, which is about to begin soon. Frequently, Catholic high schools and colleges offer in their spring semesters some sort of program or course for the continuing education of Catholic adults in their Faith, usually without the customary requirements of high school or college student status or degree completion. There may well be such an opportunity for us, especially one which will help us to share wisdom with others in our community, as a religious education staff member, CCD teacher, or the like. Of course, those who are parents can specially benefit from whatever preparation will help them to train their own children for Christian life, particularly in preparing for the sacraments such as Holy Communion, Confession or Confirmation.

Sacrifice is necessary

Any of the examples just mentioned will necessitate some sacrifice of time and energy, and perhaps even some monetary expense, on the part of each of us. This is as necessary to our lives as members of the Church as it is for us to read the daily newspapers or listen to the news broadcasts if we would be informed members of civil society. And the religious society to which we belong as Christians is one of the greatest importance. As Paul tells the Ephesians: "God chose us in him before the world began to be holy and blameless in his sight, to be full of love ... that all might praise the divine favor he has bestowed on us in his beloved."

Let us then share and celebrate and bear witness to the wisdom that has been given us in the Person of the Word of God made flesh, our Lord Jesus the Christ.

Epiphany

The first reading of today's liturgy, from the latter part of the Old Testament book named for Isaiah, envisions not merely the Jerusalem of history but also a new Jerusalem which is to come. This is carried out in the Responsorial Psalm and in the New Testament readings of today's liturgy as well: the kingdom that is promised to Israel will be greater than Israel could ever dream.

We are well through a Christmas season which, once more, has brought to our homes and our communities the familiar signs of this traditional time of year. In some families, there are special customs which are repeated Christmas after Christmas. Throughout the years these never change much, even though the circumstances of the families in question will necessarily undergo much change—some of it unhappy or turbulent. In fact these familiar customs often provide us with some stability in the face of change, or despite it.

Christmas and comforting familiarity

Many of us, as we grow older, and even move away from the places we call "home," try to preserve as much as we can those customs and associations which mean Christmas, and which mean stability even in a world which seems to change so much around us. For a great many of us, the Christmas season, up until this feast of Epiphany, is a celebration of our own identity which remains substantially the same even when we are buffeted by hectic and sometimes unwelcome change. We may tend to feel that it "just isn't Christmas time" unless customs are observed in a certain way which was learned by us as small children. We may think the holidays have lost their character if we cannot see them observed in the manner which is most familiar and most comforting to us personally.

Epiphany can be unsettling

The message of this Epiphany celebration, though, takes us in a somewhat different direction, and one which at first might appear a bit unsettling. For the Scriptural readings for the Epiphany Mass all have to do with universality of worship in the same Lord. In the Old Testament reading, we see how people shall come for miles, from everywhere, to bring their offerings to the same God. This is surely the key to the story of the Gospel narrative according to Matthew. And in Paul's pastoral letter to the Church at Ephesus, we are reminded how the kingdom of God is meant not to be for one people or group alone, but for all, ". . . members of the same body and sharers of the promise. . . ."

Religious expressions legitimately differ

We who treasure our own family or community celebrations during this Christmas season might not appreciate adequately the different religious expressions of people who worship the same Jesus as Lord, and celebrate the same saving Incarnation. Those of us who belong to the Roman Rite of the Catholic Church are about ninety-five percent of the membership of the Church united with the Pope of Rome. But we constitute only one of many *rites*. There are over a dozen major rites—and many more if we count each subdivision among the rites. Every one of these is as licit and legitimate as the Roman Rite. Their customs might be quite different. Their liturgical forms might seem to us exotic or even bizarre. All the same, they have as

much claim as we do to identify as members of the Roman
Catholic Church. Their priests commonly are bearded, and
often married men. Such a thing might seem strange to the
Western Catholic! But these are members of the very same
Church! In fact, they represent some of the regions which seem
to be implied in today's Gospel story concerning the travellers
from the east.

Unity in diversity

Those of us who are fond of our own Christmas-time
customs are not usually asked to forsake our own observance
of the holidays in favor of someone else's. We are generally
allowed to preserve those rituals and procedures which are especially dear to ourselves or our families. But we are encouraged
to know, understand and appreciate the customs of other families and other people in other places. The same principle applies
to the various rites of the Catholic Church. We are not asked
for the sake of unity to forsake the diversity which allows us
our own rite. By the same token, we do not ask others for the
sake of unity to forsake the same diversity which guarantees
them the integrity of *their* own rites and their own demonstra-
tions of Christian spirituality.

The term "Catholic" as applied to the Church means "universal," or pertaining to what the community of faith has always
believed, essentially, in all places and times. This is why so many
different rites, sharing the same beliefs, can demonstrate a
variety of external rituals and symbols and still be essentially
Catholic. There are, of course, those communions which do
not share our belief in the ultimate authority of the Bishop of
Rome, our Holy Father the Pope, as successor to Peter. These
communions are called schismatic, like the Orthodox Christians
who worship in the same rites as do many Christians in union
with Rome, or the members of the Anglican communion (commonly called Episcopalian in the United States). But they have
some claim on the term "Catholic" even though they are not
Roman Catholic or united under the authority of Rome.

As we conclude a season of celebration in honor of the taking-flesh of the Word of God, Jesus, we are in a particularly appropriate position to see how the Word is incarnate in the Church. We can see, too, that the Christian community is not one. There are those who would claim to preserve the Catholic tradition in ways which we as Roman Catholics would see as incomplete. Yet these, as Anglicans and Eastern Orthodox, are our brothers and sisters in a special way. We can see that to be *Roman* Catholic need not mean to be Roman *Rite*. The Church has room for diversity, precisely in the context of her overall unity. This is a good time to reaffirm our faith in the Holy Spirit, who gives life to the Church, and who will help those of us who submit to his authority in the bringing together of all who believe in one Lord, one faith and one baptism.

(The above may be particularly appropriate in preparation for the Church Unity Octave.)

Sunday after January 6 (Baptism of the Lord):

The first reading, from the Old Testament Book of Isaiah, high-lights the image of the "servant of the Lord," whose suffering will be a cause of salvation for the People of God. In the second selection, from the New Testament book of the Acts of the Apostles, the universality of salvation and the necessity of baptism in the Spirit are brought out. In the account of the Gospel according to Mark, we see again the necessity of baptism in the Spirit.

One thing is made clear above all others in the Biblical readings selected by the Church for today's liturgical celebration: each one of us must be baptized in the Spirit.

Several types of baptism

John the Baptist, according to the Gospel account we read today, was quick to distinguish between his own baptism administered at the Jordan and the baptism in the Spirit which would be part of the New Covenant in Jesus. Before that New Covenant, there were several types of baptismal rituals, for different purposes, among the Jews. None of these, even the particularly important baptism of John himself, was baptism in the Spirit, in the New Covenant which was to center in Jesus. This baptism in the Spirit could take place only when the New Covenant was itself firmly established, after the mission, death/resurrection/ascension of Jesus the Christ, and the sending of the Spirit by Jesus and God the Father to give life to the Church. Once the old Covenant had been fulfilled in the New, this baptism in the Spirit could take place, and would be necessary for the salvation of all men.

Baptism must be chosen

It will be necessary to point out two things concerning this baptism of the Spirit. The first is that such a baptism can be chosen only by those who are in fact able to make the choice in the first place. In other words, if someone is prevented from choosing baptism in the Holy Spirit by circumstances—for instance, ignorance of the Faith which requires this—they can still be saved. But for those of us who are able to know and choose this baptism, it is necessary. Such a baptism is necessarily sacramental. It is a sign. It is a sign of our sharing in the death/resurrection of Jesus, as members now of his Body in the world, the Church. Someone who is baptized in the Spirit is baptized not only into Jesus, but into his Church which receives its very life from the Holy Spirit sent by Jesus united with God the Father.

Baptism and Confirmation

Secondly, the presence of the Holy Spirit is necessary in the life of every Christian. In the documents of the New Testament which describe the life of the Church in its infancy, we know that one's initiation into the community of faith was considered incomplete until he had received the Holy Spirit. So it was that initiation into the Body of Christ had to be completed by the giving of the Holy Spirit, under the authority of first the Apostles and later their successors. While there was not always a clear-cut distinction between these two in the history of the Church, this factor gave rise to what we regard today as the two specific Sacraments of Baptism and Confirmation, both needed for one's full initiation into the worshipping community of Christians which we call the Church.

There are a variety of historical and theological theories about the origins of various baptismal and confirmation rituals during the earliest years of the Church's life. There are, too, a number of pastoral approaches, in various places, concerning the administration of these sacraments of initiation. In one locality, the bishops and pastors may elect one way of seeing that the members of the Church are baptized in the Spirit, and are initiated more fully in the same Spirit in confirmation. In another place, the practice may differ somewhat. In any case, the need for initiation in the Holy Spirit is basic to one's identity as a member of the Body of Christ which is the Church.

Initiation to activity

Another element which will be seen in the sacraments of initiation, as we are coming to call them with increasing frequency today, is that they make one a vital and active member of a worshipping community, where initiation into the death/resurrection of Jesus is completed, time after time, by participation in the liturgy of the Holy Eucharist. Initiation into Christ means not passivity, but *activity* of various sorts, the most important of which will be participation in the eucharistic celebration of the Church.

Finally, we do well to remember with special emphasis the fact that the initiation of a member into community in Christ is an initiation into Christian *service*. Each of us, in the baptism in the Spirit and the gift of the Spirit, is called upon to prepare for and execute *service* in the name of the Lord, for the salvation of mankind and the glory of God, "... to open the eyes of the blind, to bring out prisoners from confinement, and from the dungeon, those who live in darkness." This is the message we will bring to all men and women, as a sign of the life of the Spirit that should be in us all.

Sundays "of the year" after this first one follow at the back of this volume, according to the scheme of the Roman Lectionary.

First Sunday of Lent

The image of the flood, introduced in this liturgy by the first reading (Gn 9:8-15), is reiterated in the second (1 P 3:18-22), where the waters of the flood are juxtaposed with the waters of Baptism in the New Covenant. The image of baptismal water leads to consideration of Jesus, who was baptized by John in the Jordan, preparing to undertake his earthly ministry, as in today's Gospel (Mk 1:12-15).

Food for thought

As usual, the lessons of the Bible chosen for reading in the day's liturgy are complex, and any one of their implications could give us much food for thought. Let us concentrate on one of them, as particularly appropriate for this First Sunday of Lent, and that is the element of preparation, as implied in today's Gospel reading.

In preparation for his earthly mission during his public life of ministry, we are told, Jesus went to the desert to fast and pray, and there he was put to the test, which he passed by refusing the allurements of Satan. It is interesting to note how the New Testament tells us that even the Son of God did not begin his work without some contemplation by way of preparation.

Preparation

Most of us consider the major events in our lives important

enough to warrant some serious and thorough preparation: most careers, trades and professions involve some sort of formal training or education; many social events in our lives require some kind of getting-ready, and so forth. Jesus' earthly ministry in his public life required preparation, not only through the visible commitment shown in his baptism by John in the Jordan, but also in prayer, meditation and fasting.

Easter is most important

The most important thing we as Christians do is to celebrate Easter. We do this not only on Easter Sunday or at Easter time, but every day of our Christian life, in a variety of ways. Our thoughts, words and deeds, if we are truly Christian, are all reflections or celebrations of the fact that Christ who died is now risen and will come again.

This celebration of the Easter mystery, and therefore of our own sharing in Jesus' saving death and resurrection, will manifest itself in many ways, including our liturgical worship, our life as a Christian community, and our own individual lives of faith, hope and love in the name of Jesus. But this cannot really take place without preparation. And while there is necessarily a certain amount of interior preparation at all times in Christian life, there is a special opportunity for preparation during this season of Lent. This is why the Church calls to mind the image of Jesus, in the Gospel, removing himself from the rest of the world so as to go into the desert to fast and pray.

The notion of fasting has undergone some change in recent years. The previous regulations in the Church, of fast and of abstinence from meat, have been made more flexible, so as to allow for a number of forms of penance, and not only the ones we were previously accustomed to. But the basic principle of fasting—both in its previous form and in the modified discipline we know today—remains the same: to remove ourselves for a time from the patterns of life we are used to on a regular basis, so as to become less dependent on the familiar, and in such a way as to help us think in flexible and open terms about who we are and where we are going.

Retreat

Most of us are unable to emulate the example of Jesus in today's Gospel by literally going into the desert. There has developed in the Church the traditional practice of going on retreat in some form or another, and many have done this and continue this practice—again, perhaps in some modified form. But even if we are not able to physically take leave of our everyday surroundings, there should be some opportunity for each of us to draw back for a while, even a little while, from our day-to-day lives and reflect on our goals in our Christian lives, and the obstacles that stand in the way of these goals, as well as the ways in which we can better work *towards* those goals.

In one place or another, we may find an opportunity to take part in a religious-education series, a discussion group, a Bible study session, or something else that will help illuminate our lives as members of Jesus' Body on earth, the Church. These are all ways of preparation for our continuing celebration of Easter, and our continuing living of life in Christ. When we do this, we do as Jesus did in preparation for his own ministry on earth, in which we now have an active part.

(Obviously, this is a good opportunity for mentioning any special parish, diocesan or regional religious education programs taking place during Lent.)

Second Sunday of Lent

The classic story of Abraham and Isaac (Gn 22:1-2, 9, 10-13, 15-18) is followed in the second reading (Rm 8:31-34), illustrating the same notion: trust in God. The basis for such trust is further illustrated in the Gospel (Mk 9:2-10), although the passage intimates that the disciples did not at that time fully comprehend what was being communicated to them.

Tests

We read in last week's liturgy about Jesus preparing for his earthly ministry by fasting and praying in the desert, and how he was put to the test by Satan. The tests Jesus was put to had to do with temptations we all face at various times: the temptations towards excessive dependence on material goods and earthly power. We might wonder how each of us might respond to such tests, which have ways of coming up, time and time again, in our everyday lives. One answer which we might well consider is presented in the first two readings of our liturgy today.

The basic message of those two readings seems to be "Trust God." This is clearly what Abraham did, following God's commands to the point of being ready to sacrifice his beloved son. The only way this could be done was by virtue of great faith, the kind of faith Paul describes in the second of today's readings: "If God is for us, who can be against us?" The meaning is clear: Only God and his provident love are necessary for man, who needs only to respond appropriately to grace.

Let go!

Put another way, the thrust of today's Scriptural lessons is: "Let go!" Let go of the things that weigh you down, and which keep you from living to the fullest possible extent in the life of Christ. But, of course, this is easily said, and not so easily done. We come to apprehend the Gospel itself with so much excess baggage to begin with, it seems at times a wonder that we are even able to be ready listeners to the word of God in the first place.

The story of Abraham is the story of a man who let go of his homeland, and who is prepared—if God really demands it—to let go of his son, and of all his preconceived notions concerning what will happen. Abraham would be held up as an example for the rest of time because of the faith demonstrated in this story. But most of us feel inadequate by comparison.

It happens gradually for most

Perhaps, for most of us, Abraham is not an appropriate term of comparison at the outset. Maybe it makes more sense to use ourselves as we are, as a term of comparison with ourselves as we would wish to be, as Christians. In that regard, perhaps we can think of shedding our excess baggage not all at once, but piece by piece. The Epistle to the Romans, from which we read today, is one of many places where Paul, in the New Testament, seems to realize that those Christians in his charge will not always understand everything right away, and will have to be taught and sometimes even prodded continually, and a little patiently. The same principle is implied in the Gospel narrative, where we get the idea that Peter, James and John did not grasp the full import of what was revealed to them.

If we apply to ourselves the same patience which the Apostles and the Lord would apply, then we are perhaps looking at things more realistically. And then we are in a position to ask ourselves which pieces of excess baggage in our lives are heaviest, and most in need of being shed, and which ones could be shed first, thereby lightening the burden.

Which attitudes, which ways of thinking and looking at things, which habits or patterns, which things keep me from being more of a Christian? Is there a long-standing grudge against one of my neighbors—one of my relatives, friends or co-workers? Have I become excessively dependent on certain material goods? Am I perhaps too insistent on my own point of view in some matters? Are there patterns of behavior that are pleasing to me for my own selfish reasons, but harmful to those around me? Do I refuse to see other people in terms of themselves, for who they are, and not just as I think they *should* be?

Excess baggage

Most of us have one or more of these kinds of excess baggage, and each of us can ask himself or herself, honestly, which piece of excess baggage weighs us down heaviest, and which ones could be shed first so as to lighten the over-all load. Letting go may be difficult for us, much the same as it's difficult to leave some things behind when we move. But we also know, as in moving to a new place, that there are some things we must leave unless we want them to impede our progress, and maybe keep us from moving, altogether. Lent is an especially good time for trying to see what we can let go of.

Third Sunday of Lent

The first reading outlines the Decalogue as given to Moses (Ex 20:1-17), and both the New Testament readings (1 Cor 1:22-25; Jn 2:13-25) stress that the Law for its own sake, in terms that are external or superficial, should not be the focal point of man's attention. As noted in the Gospel, Jesus' own person and teachings, culminating in his resurrection, will supplant the Law of old, although it will remain for us a useful way of knowing Jesus' own demands on us.

A dilemma

The readings of today's liturgy pose a certain dilemma for us, it appears. On the one hand, some stress is given to the importance of the Law. On the other hand, Jesus is described in the Gospel as warning us not to put too much emphasis on external signs. Paul's words in his Epistle to the Corinthians, also, warn that the externals are not so important as the main thing: "Christ is the power of God and the wisdom of God." It is this Christ whom we see depicted as rebuking the money-changers in the temple, although all the external standards of priorities and proprieties at that time dictated against his action.

What are we to make of these things? On the one hand, we know that the externals are not the main thing. On the other hand, we realize our human need for some external guideposts to point out the way to us. On the one hand, we realize that structures are not everything. On the other hand, we know that structures can help to achieve some very important things in our lives, including our spiritual lives in particular.

Confusion has worsened

Our confusion in matters like these has perhaps been made worse over the past several years, since a number of speakers and writers have told us that moral law as we have come to know it is not so important as the particular *situation* in which a moral law might apply. This approach, or "situation ethics" as it is commonly called, might seem at first to be an excuse for those who do not want to follow God's moral teachings. And, if we are to be honest, we must admit that there are some people who have used "situation ethics" for just such a purpose, so as to rationalize and say "Well, *this* law doesn't apply to me in my situation; I can be considered excepted from the obligation!" Every one of us, at one time or another, might like to have that kind of rationalization in our favor, in the face of the difficult obligations of moral law.

"Situation ethics"

But there is another side to the question. While it is true that the approach known as "situation ethics" can be used as an easy way out, the serious scholars and churchmen who propose this notion do not intend that. What they intend, rather, is that we consider, in each situation, just what our obligations are, even beyond what might be our responsibility according to the letter of the law. To many Catholics, this is not really so terribly new. Just think of the Commandments which we hear again today, and which we have read and heard for some years in our moral training. We know that, in terms of these commandments, there are obligations over and above those of the letter of the law, and which can bind us in line with the *spirit* of the law. The Commandment against killing obliges us not only to refrain from murder—which we generally do anyway—but from needless harm to the lives of others and ourselves, either by some action or by some omission on our own part. It requires that we take proper care of ourselves, and those around us, physically, and also emotionally, to whatever extent reasonably possible. By way of extension, this Commandment is very much in tune with the current awareness of the environment, or ecology, and would prompt us to respect and protect all forms of life, human and otherwise, as part of our reverence for God the creator of all.

There are other good examples, of course, but the point is made: the letter of the law is a guideline, calling upon us to consider our own obligations seriously. If we are honest with ourselves, we will likely discover that our obligations go far beyond the letter of the law. This is what Jesus seems to have acted on when he rose up in righteous indignation against those who defiled the temple, despite the fact that the authorities seemed to permit their doing so.

Dangerous extremes

But with all this emphasis on the interpretation of one's own obligations, there are obvious dangers which we can see: one is being scrupulous, or feeling responsible for more obligations than we reasonably should; the other extreme, laxity, would have us excusing ourselves at every turn, in a manner that would be all out of line with objective proportion or reality. At every time of year, but especially Lent, it is good to remember that our own "examination of conscience" can take place with recourse to the counsel of a regular spiritual director or confessor, in connection with the sacrament of Penance.

Fourth Sunday of Lent

Today's first reading from the Old Testament (2 Ch 36:14-17, 19-23) highlights the destruction of Judaism's religious institutions in their external forms, as a fulfillment of God's chastisement of his people who ignored his word through the prophets; a contrast between those who hear God's word and those who do not is offered us by today's Gospel (Jn 3:14-21). Between these two, Paul's Epistle (Ep 2:4-10) reminds us that man's salvation is the work of God, not man.

Self-examination

In the liturgies of previous weeks during this season of the liturgical year, we have seen how Lent is a particularly appropriate time for a sort of personal moral and spiritual inventory— a good time to take stock of ourselves, and of those things which may stand in the way of our becoming closer to God and to each other.

If we have been undergoing this type of self-examination with any seriousness, we realize that this is at times a difficult and demanding process, and we may feel that there has been quite a bit of effort on our own part. We might even feel, if truth be told, that we have some occasion to give ourselves the proverbial "pat on the back." In one way, that is not out of order. If we have been making an honest attempt at self-examination or self-improvement, during Lent or, for that matter, at any other time, we owe it to ourselves to give ourselves a bit of encouragement. Effort without encouragement is seldom productive of the desired results.

Smugness is a danger

At the same time, there is a danger behind that "pat on the back," and it is this: we might tend to become just a little smug, by way of comparison with some others we know. After all, those of us who regularly worship at the Eucharist are a rather small number in terms of the total populace. A number of years ago, a prominent sociologist, Father Joseph Fichter, called people who fulfill their weekly obligation of Mass by the name "nuclear Catholics," meaning those who comprise a *nucleus* in the Church, a central core, as distinct from those who are not in that inner core. Since Father Fichter's initial use of that term, the number of so-called "nuclear Catholics" has not grown in proportion, but indeed diminished in proportion, to the total Catholic population, let alone the total population in general. So the very fact of our being here, week after week, can give us occasion to compare ourselves with others, and perhaps to become a little too self-satisfied or smug. We might tend to feel that we have *earned* salvation, because our own efforts have been so much greater than those of the people around us. In fact, if we were to speak of the others we know, who have not done as we have done, in terms of today's Gospel passage, there would be a number of things we might be tempted to say about them by way of contrast with ourselves, which would make them look pretty bad and ourselves pretty good.

Grace is a gift

But we must not ever lose sight of the fact that men can respond to the divine invitation to friendship only to the extent that we understand it as being extended to them, and only insofar as they are blessed with the grace to respond to it. Even despite a number of outward appearances that may be confusing or misleading to the outside observer—family background, education, or whatever—there are perhaps many who do not embrace the person and teachings of Jesus in his Church because they have not received or recognized that invitation from the Lord—which we call grace—to do so.

If we want to see the situation in proper perspective we would do well to heed the words of Paul, in his Epistle to the Ephesians, from today's liturgical readings: It is owing to (God's) favor that salvation is (ours) through faith. This is not (our) own doing, it is God's gift. In fact, our word *grace* in English, from the Latin *gratia*, actually means a gift given freely, without being earned or deserved. This is what grace means: God's gift to man, which man can never earn or deserve, and which only God can give. And the ways in which grace will be given by God, and received by men in various circumstances, will be beyond our own understanding.

This means we have every reason to continue living in thanksgiving to God for his goodness, as manifest in the saving presence of Jesus in the Church, but never to be smug or to hold others in contempt. As Paul says: "By this favor you were saved. . . . This is not your own doing, it is God's gift; neither is it a reward for anything you have accomplished, so let no one pride himself on it."

Fifth Sunday of Lent

The Old Testament liturgical reading today is quite a contrast from last week's. Last week the first reading showed God's punishment of Israel; this week we see the extension of divine mercy and a new covenant (Jr 31:31-34). There is in the history of Israel a motif of death-and-resurrection, and this is brought out in today's Gospel passage (Jn 12:20-33). In the Epistle (Heb 5:7-9), we see how Jesus, truly man as well as truly divine, needed to offer prayer to God the Father.

Death and resurrection

The Old Testament readings of the previous week and today, taken together, show us the destruction of many of the external forms of ritual worship which had become dear to the Israelites. In today's passage from the book of the prophet Jeremiah, we see God as loving father being willing to make a new covenant, even though the Covenant he made with Israel was not kept by the people he had chosen. Israel as it existed had to undergo a kind of death before it could live again, the Scriptures tell us. In the Gospel, the idea is stressed that this theme of death-and-resurrection is a part of life in general, and of spiritual life in particular.

During this season of Lent, we have had occasion to consider those things in our lives which we would do well to continue, and those which we should discontinue, in terms of what helps us to grow as Christians, and to come closer to God and to each other in a Christian community of faith, hope and charity. This is something, of course, which we should be doing not only during Lent, but at all times. And we will find, if we consider these matters seriously, that when some things terminate, others that are more helpful are able to take their place, that certain old ways can give way to new ones, and that some things that may have been very good in our lives at some previous time need to be replaced by something else that makes more sense today.

Self-examination for the Church

It should not surprise us that the Church as a total community should go through a process like this as well. And, of course, that is just what has been happening throughout the history of the Church. In the first century of Christian history, we see how the Apostles did this at Jerusalem, when it was decided to admit Gentiles to the Church without making them embrace the Mosaic Law, and also how the Apostles did this in selecting the first deacons to minister to the needs of the Christian community. In later centuries we have seen the same type of thing in the Church's history, including the reforms of the Lateran Councils and the Council of Trent, the establishment of new and better systems for Church organization, education of the clergy, regulation of religious-order life, and the encouragement of eucharistic devotion, Biblical studies, the lay apostolate, and so on.

The past several years in our own century have seen an especially dramatic period of self-evaluation and renewal in the life of the Church. Since the early 1960's we have seen introduced the vernacular in the Mass and other sacramental rites, the increased participation of the laity in both the liturgy and in the decision-making processes of the Christian community, the expansion of ministry to include permanent deacons, extraordinary ministers of the Eucharist, and others, and a certain flexibility in the fulfillment of obligations to worship regularly in the Mass (meaning Sunday or holy day Mass may be anticipated on the vigil) and to make sacrifices during penitential times like Lent.

Flexibility can be difficult

The changes we have just mentioned have been difficult, in many cases, for a significant number of people who have been used to doing things in a different way. It can be very difficult to change a familiar and comfortable way of doing things, especially when the reasons why we should do so may not be immediately clear to us. We often tend to feel that it would be so much easier, and would make so much more sense, just to leave things as they are, rather than try to change established patterns.

But sometimes there are substantial reasons for allowing one way of doing things—even a very good and admirable way —to make room for a new way that will be even better. This means that something old has to give way to something new, and this will be like a kind of death, like the death of old attitudes for new in the history of Israel, or the death of a grain of wheat so that it may give fruit. And in both those examples, as in the very death and resurrection of Jesus himself, and of his followers who share it, what appears to be death is in reality the gateway to new life. That is the meaning of Lent, and of Easter, and of all our Christian lives.

Palm Sunday (Passion Sunday)

Today's first liturgical reading is the third "Servant song" from Isaiah, stressing the messianic image of the "suffering servant" whose trials will be salvific for the People of God. This is followed by Paul's words to the Philippians, reminding Jesus' followers of his humiliation for our sake—which, in the way of Christian paradox, occasions men to adore him, then the Passion according to Mark.

A balance

We have tended, in the past, to emphasize the cross of Christ a great deal. Some theologians and liturgists, after the restoration of the Holy Week liturgy in the 1950's, felt that we were arriving at a better balance than we had before. We would now emphasize the cross, still, but we would give greater stress to the central mystery of salvation, which is not the cross in itself, but the resurrection in which Jesus' death culminates. We would then be avoiding the dangers of emphasizing the cross too much. On the other hand, there has been the danger of stressing the cross too little.

The cross as symbol

Today's Biblical readings call on us to be mindful of the cross, not only as a sign of Jesus' suffering for the sake of mankind, but moreover as a symbol of and for Christian humility. As Paul tells us in his admonition to the Philippians: "Your attitude must be Christ's . . . he emptied himself and took the form of a slave . . . and it was thus that he humbled himself. . . ." There will always be a need for this attitude among the followers of the Lord who ". . . did not deem equality with God something to be grasped at."

The true meaning of humility

Yet humility does not consist of only thinking of those things which lessen our inflated self-images. Humility also includes things which build up our self-images when they are not positive enough. Humility, in a word, includes emphasizing our own dignity. Nothing could stress each Christian's dignity more powerfully than the knowledge that each of us shares in Jesus' resurrection, just as we share in his death.

Saving element in unity

These elements of Jesus' saving activity—his death and resurrection—cannot be viewed in isolation from each other. They must be seen as a unity. For this reason it is particularly important that we pay attention to all of the liturgical services for this Holy Week, beginning with this Mass of Palm or Passion Sunday, as it is called, and culminating in the celebration of Easter. A most fitting way of doing this, if at all possible, is participation in the most solemn of liturgies throughout the entire Church year, in the Easter Vigil Mass. And, of course, there will be other important liturgies during this holy season: the special celebration of the Eucharist on Maundy or Holy Thursday, and the liturgical service of Good Friday. In addition, there will be the Sundays and weekdays when we continue to utter, again and again, the *Alleluia!* that belongs to the Easter season.

Let us take this reading of the passion of our Lord as an invitation to come to know him better, that we may know ourselves better as well, in the liturgy of the Church.

Holy Thursday:
Mass of the Lord's Supper

The first reading, from Exodus, shows how the keeping of ritual Law was seen as essential to the Israelites' remembrance of who they were as a people and as a religious society and what their destiny would be in the divine plan we call Salvation-History. The second reading, from Paul's first letter to the Christian community at Corinth, reflects the law of the New Covenant in Christ in its focal point of the celebration of the new Passover feast, the Eucharist. Finally, the Gospel selection from the account according to John shows how the acting-out of the Eucharistic sacrament is seen in terms of the sort of service and charity towards men which Jesus showed his disciples at the Last Supper.

Rediscovery of the Sacred

We are beginning to rediscover, in our time, the importance of ritual and the importance of the sacred. There was a time, not so long ago, when we tended to celebrate what some called "the secular city" and to feel that nothing was necessarily more sacred than anything else. All was sacred and all was secular, in such a way that we could hardly distinguish between the two. In an atmosphere like that, we are likely hard put to recognize the *specially* sacred. As even the author of *The Secular City* seems to have admitted lately, we are in danger of becoming impoverished a bit in our apprehension of the divine and our celebrations of meaning in life, if we take secularity to extremes.

In our own time, we are coming to re-emphasize the sacred as distinct and special. We are coming to re-emphasize, as well, the importance of celebrating the sacred in ritual action. In this context, we will see the Eucharist as being of singular importance at *any* time, but especially on this feast of Holy or Maundy Thursday, when we celebrate and commemorate the very *beginnings* of the Christian Eucharist.

Not in a vacuum

The Eucharist as we know it did not develop in a complete vacuum. There was ritual before there was a Eucharist. And we see the ritual reflected, in part, in the first reading of this liturgy, dealing with the Passover ritual. Just as the Jews had a special meal to celebrate their liberation from Egypt, Christians have a special meal—the Eucharist—to celebrate liberation in Christ from sin and death, and entry into a life of grace in Jesus' resurrection.

The death of Jesus was a death to sin once and for all. His resurrection gives new meaning to death and life. This is the central mystery of the Christian Faith, or if you will the "feature story" in the Good News of the Gospel. So we celebrate this fact with all the importance we can bring to our ritual of Eucharist, especially on this day which commemorates the Eucharist's origin.

Sacrament of unity

One thing which we celebrate, in a particularly solemn way, in the Eucharist, is the fact of the Eucharist as *sacrament of unity* in the Church. We see that those who are united in Christ sacramentally must be united in him in fraternal charity, concern and service towards one another. This is why we have in our Gospel, according to John, the story of Jesus' washing his disciples' feet at the meal they celebrated together. The ritual of the washing of the feet has become a part of the liturgy for this day, and is observed throughout the world in many places. It should be part of our Eucharistic ritual every day, at least spiritually, in that we always remember, when celebrating the Eucharist, that we should be celebrating our dedication to one another in the Body of Christ. And when we come together to make Eucharist, as solemnly and with as much importance as possible, we strengthen the very identity and unity of that Body.

Good Friday

The liturgy of Good Friday recalls the image of the "suffering servant" of Isaiah, whose identity is fulfilled in the redemptive passion and death of Jesus. This service is special, in that it is mediatorship, or priesthood, on behalf of mankind to God the Father, as brought out in the second reading from the Epistle to the Hebrews (commonly attributed to Paul). The events of this priestly activity are recounted in the Passion narrative according to John.

We notice that the liturgy today is different from the liturgy of all the other days of the Church calendar throughout the year. Its form is different, and yet its basic meaning is the same. We are still celebrating the priesthood of Jesus the Christ, and his presence in the world through his Body the Church. Moreover, we are celebrating his presence in the Church through the Eucharist.

A priest is a mediator

Priesthood is particularly emphasized in our second reading, from the Epistle to the Hebrews. It is here that we see the meaning of what it is to be a priest: it means to be a mediator between God and man, bringing the one closer to the other. Obviously, the only one who can fully claim the title of priest, then, is Jesus. He will have claim to this title, surely, far beyond whatever claim is laid by the "high priests" of the Gospel account, like Caiaphas. And even the priests of our own Christian community have no priesthood on their own, but only a sharing in the one true priesthood which belongs to no one but Jesus. And Jesus' priesthood—in whom his representatives and followers would share—is based on suffering, like that described in today's first reading from the prophetic book named for Isaiah in the Old Testament: ". . . it was our infirmities that he bore, our sufferings that he endured, while we thought of him as stricken, as one smitten by God and afflicted." The priest of Christ will have to be a servant of the community in all things.

All of what has just been mentioned could make sense for ordained priests. But it can hardly stop there. For we know that all Christians, ordained or not, have some measure of sharing in Jesus' one true priesthood. Therefore, while it is perfectly legitimate to expect that the ordained priest share in the suffering and service of Christ's priesthood, we must acknowledge that all who follow Jesus, and thus all who have some share in his priesthood or mediatorship, are called to share in his suffering and his service for the sake of mankind, that man and God might be brought closer together.

Suffering is unavoidable

We have had reason to see that Christians hardly *seek* suffering unnecessarily. But, when suffering is unavoidably a part of the Christian mission, it is viewed as pointing to a higher goal, which is the kingdom of Christ. This will be a real part of every Christian's life, in one fashion or another. And when being a mediator between God and man becomes difficult for any of us—as it certainly does for all of us—because of rebuke or hardship or simply that everyday frustration that gnaws at one from inside, we can remember what we are told by the Epistle to the Hebrews: ". . . let us hold fast to our profession of faith. For we do not have a priest who is unable to sympathize with our weakness, but one who was tempted in every way that we are, yet never sinned. So let us confidently approach the throne of grace to receive mercy and favor and to find help in time of need."

And let us, therefore, have recourse often to the sacrament of the Eucharist, in the liturgy of the Church day after day, for it is here that we especially witness to and share in the priesthood, the mediatorship, of the one true high priest, Jesus, "... the source of eternal salvation for all who obey him."

Easter (The Resurrection of the Lord):
Easter Vigil

The readings assigned to the Easter Vigil service total nine, in an attempt to provide both variety and depth in exposition of the themes pertinent to the Salvation-History which culminates in the death/resurrection of the Word made flesh. Circumstances may necessitate the reduction of readings to a total of as few as four (including Epistle and Gospel); in any case Ex 14:15-15:1 should always be included.* It might be well to consider not only the elements of time and other conditions, but also the congregation's receptivity to Biblical literature, specifically the Old Testament, in selecting the readings for this service. At the same time, lack of receptivity on the part of a congregation should be viewed not so much as a reason to condense readings as a reason to increase understanding of and receptivity to the literature of the Bible, and in particular the Old Testament, in the congregation in question. The homiletic materials presented below will find themselves helpful in proportion to the selection of readings for the service.

The Old Testament readings for the service are all illustrative of ways in which God made himself known to the Israelites, throughout Salvation-history, as a God who would be present in the lives of his People to be of constant assistance to them.

---

* Lectionary for Mass, q. v., p. 9.

The Israelites, as we have seen before in the Old Testament, have tended to personalize a variety of evidences of God's intervention in their behalf, even the beginning of life itself in Creation (Gn 1:1-2:2). The responsibility of the People of God in response to divine initiative is acceptance of and carrying out of God's will (Gn 22:1-18), which will culminate in God's guidance of his People out of bondage into freedom in a new life (Ex 14:15-15:1), which will not be lost despite the infidelities of the People of Israel to their God (Is 54:5-14), although God —particularly through his prophetic messengers—will need to remind his People of their identity and their obligations (Ba 3: 9-15, 32; 4:4) if they are to continue as his People and as evidence of his presence in Salvation-history.

The ultimate involvement of God in Salvation-History, the making-flesh of the Word of God, culminates in the sharing of men in the death/resurrection of the God-man Jesus (Rm 6: 3-11), first made known to the joyous followers of Jesus after his crucifixion (Mt 28:1-10).

Easter Sunday

The first reading selected for today's liturgy is in line with Augustine's maxim Moritur Christus ut fiat ecclesia *(Christ dies that the Church might live). Immediately, this Easter service begins with an account of the Church (in the form of Peter's preaching) that lived after the death and resurrection of Jesus. Likewise, the second reading (Col 3:1-4 or 1 Cor 5:6-8) exhibits the vitality of the Church in the first century, calling upon the members of Christ to be lively witnesses to his Person and purpose. Finally, the Gospel reading for the Mass (Jn 20:1-9)** is a demonstration of the joy of Jesus' followers upon the realization of his victory over death.*

Signs of life

If there is any message that comes to us through the words of the Easter liturgy, it is a theme of life or vitality. Surely, in the Easter Vigil liturgy, there is a celebration of all things living and created: water, the bees who make the wax of candles, all the earth joining in the *Alleluia* of the most sacred night of the year. And in the Mass of Easter Sunday morning, we celebrate not only the triumph of Jesus over death and sin, but also the very life of his body in the world, the Church.

Usually, the signs of the times around us will call to mind

**Note the alternatives that may be used according to the *Lectionary for Mass*, p. 104.

a spirit of vitality as well. We need think only of the Easter lily, of the changing seasons, as signs of rebirth and newness in even the world around us. But, we all know, it is not always that way. Sometimes, the climate or weather at Easter time is hardly suggestive of new life or vitality. And, even if it is, there may be circumstances in our own lives which will not lead us to shout *Alleluia!* Instead, the things going on in or around our own personal Christian lives may be even more discouraging than the most somber of penitential liturgies, more intimidating than the most dramatic of the old "fire-and-brimstone" sermons, more discouraging than any image we can conjure up here and now.

Meaning despite discouragement

It is precisely in and for circumstances like that, that Easter has its greatest meaning. Easter is not a feast which depends on fine weather or joyful dispositions. Easter, rather, is a mystery on which all *other* things depend. Christ is risen, and Christ will come again. And if our Easter liturgy should happen to be celebrated against a background of dark and foreboding sites—physically or emotionally—the Easter mystery is nonetheless the central facet of our Faith. If our Easter liturgy should happen to be celebrated when we fear the loss of a loved one, or when we have just buried someone dear and close to us, is this any less reason for the Easter celebration? On the contrary, it provides us an even greater reason to celebrate the fact that all who die in Christ as members of his body shall rise in him, sharing a new life in grace, united with Father, Son and Holy Spirit. We celebrate the fact, as the Easter Sequence expresses, that "We know that Christ has indeed risen from the dead!"

We should be made new

The Scriptures for the Easter liturgy tell us that we should be made new from within, if we are to fully participate in the celebration of Jesus' victory over sin and death, and make this victory our own in his grace. This we can do if we are willing to set aside the sorry circumstances which may seem at times to immobilize or frighten us, and move ahead in the confident joy which should be ours as sharers in the resurrection of the Lord.

During this Easter time let us see how each of us can help make our lives new in the Risen Lord, renewed in the Spirit, and truly reflective of the joy of Christ's entire body upon his winning out once and for all over the forces of sin and death.

Second Sunday of Easter

Today's group of liturgical readings begins with the description, from the Acts of the Apostles (Ac 4:32-35) of the life of the apostolic community of faith. This theme of brotherhood in the name of Jesus is explicated further in the second reading (1 Jn 5:1-6). For those who fail in love, even after committing themselves to Jesus' message of love in life, there would be recourse to forgiveness, as described in today's Gospel (Jn 20:19-31).

Too idealistic?

The picture given us by today's first reading, from the book of the Acts of the Apostles, seems almost a little hard to believe. The statements are of such a generally optimistic character concerning the life of the first Christians that we are apt to compare these remarks against the communities we would be more familiar with, and to look at the Biblical description as being perhaps too idealistic. The same might well be true when we consider the words of the second of our readings from the New Testament; we might well wonder, how can we realize these ideals today, roughly a couple of thousand years later?

They were human too

There might be some consolation for us in the fact that the earliest followers of Jesus, like ourselves, were very much human beings, complete with faults and frailties with which we are all too familiar in our own lives. We realize this when we look at the Gospel narratives with an eye for detail: some of the Apostles were excessively concerned with rank or prestige in the worldly sense; some were thick-headed; the leader of the Apostles, Peter, showed himself a coward and a liar in a moment of panic; another, Thomas, provides us with the classic image of the doubter.

Christian leaders are not perfect

It should be clear to us from the New Testament itself that Jesus did not select perfect human beings, without flaws or weaknesses, to follow him, or even to *lead* his followers. And, every once in a while, when we read in history or even in current reports that this or that leader in the Church was or is lacking in some human virtue or another, we should not be so surprised, since these successors of the Apostles manifest the same imperfect humanity that we see so clearly in the very Apostles themselves. By the same token, we should see that our own imperfections are not unlike those of the first members of the Christian community.

We must still improve

This does not mean that we should not strive for self-improvement as Christians. The Apostles surely did, and so did the others who first embraced the person and message of Jesus the Risen Lord. So, too, do we and our religious leaders today, as has been the practice of the Christian community throughout the centuries between apostolic times and our own time. But even though we strive to be the best persons, the best Christians, we can be, we should not be surprised or discouraged if we often fail. Failure is part of human life, and it is part of the life of every Christian. It is perhaps appropriate that the same Gospel narrative which tells us of the doubting Thomas should be the one that tells us of the sacrament of reconciliation, Penance.

Another chance

The earliest Christians were typically adults, members of another religion or of no religion at all, who chose to follow the way of Jesus and to forsake anything which contradicted the Gospel. It would be presumed that this conscious and mature choice on their part would be followed. But these were human beings, capable of failure, like ourselves. And as fallible human beings, these first Christians were capable not only of minor imperfections, but even serious transgressions against the moral demands of Christian life. In light of this, today's Gospel narrative shows Jesus providing, through the Apostles, a means whereby Christians who fail to carry out the moral imperatives of the Lord can repent of their failure, and have another chance.

We know, historically, that Penance was utilized less frequently and more severely in early times than it is in recent years. No longer is the sacrament used only for serious sins, and in not too many circumstances, but it is now used to help even *good* Christians become *better* Christians, taking advantage of the forgiving grace of the Lord who loves his people, and who calls us to an ever fuller life in his Body on earth, the Church. The Apostles, and through the ages their successors, function in the name of the entire Christian community in extending the forgiving love of Jesus, and in presiding over a community of love where failure is met by forgiveness, so that each of us can say, as in the words of today's responsorial psalm: "I was hard pressed and was falling, but the Lord helped me."

Third Sunday of Easter

The first reading, once more from the Acts of the Apostles, shows Peter rebuking those among the Jews who do not follow Jesus as Messiah (Ac 3:13-15, 17-19). This apparent harshness is tempered by the second New Testament reading, where the forgiveness of the Lord—a theme in last week's readings—is underscored (1 Jn 2:1-5). The related notion of penance is brought out in the Gospel (Lk 24:35-48).

The theme of last week's readings is brought about again in today's: those who try and fail will find in Jesus a forgiving Lord, ready to be of help through the grace of the Sacraments in the community of love which is his Church.

Moral obligations are serious

This never means that we can take moral obligations lightly. Both of our first two readings today have strong words for those who do not embrace the teachings of Jesus and the obligations that come from those teachings. At the same time, there is a concrete realization of the fact that people are only human, and that for a variety of reasons, and in a variety of circumstances, we will often fail when we try to do what is right or what is best. It is against the background of such a realization that John can write: ". . . I am writing this to keep you from sin. But if anyone should sin, we have, in the presence of the Father, Jesus Christ, an intercessor who is just." This is the same Jesus who, as we read in the Gospel, will appear to the disciples so as to make clear to them his love and concern for them.

Failure is forgivable

With these things in mind, we should take very seriously not only the moral commands of Jesus, who insists that we live our lives in love and justice in all things, but also the forgiveness he extends to us when we fail in the attempt, and sincerely try to do the best we can in our own individual lives. It is hard to do either of these things . . . and it is easy to be harsh towards those who do fail in the attempt, whether they be others or ourselves.

No easy way out

Jesus would have us avoid the easy way out which ignores his teachings. But he would also have us avoid the *other* easy way out, which is to dismiss the individual who fails in trying to carry out those teachings, whether the individual be someone else that we know, or whether it be oneself. We are always ready to be hard on someone, even if the someone is oneself. We can dismiss someone else as a person who will never succeed or amount to anything because they failed, and we can do the same thing to ourselves; we can write ourselves off because we have failed in the past. But that attitude, towards either oneself or another, is a "cop-out," an escape, a sort of evasion of what is really involved.

What is really involved is a series of moral obligations, founded in love and justice, which must necessarily involve love and justice both towards others and towards ourselves. And this means allowing others, and ourselves, to have ready access to the forgiving love and grace of Christ.

In this light the Church in our time has stressed frequent or regular confession, preferably to a particular confessor with whom one can establish the proper rapport. In addition, the Church even more recently has stressed the notion of a communal celebration of this sacrament of reconciliation, so that while the confessor as delegated successor to the Apostles may exercise Christ's forgiveness of sins, those of us who make up the community of love which is Christ's Body on earth can also express Jesus' love and concern for one another. As the Bible and our theologians have been telling us, we are not isolated Christians, but a *community* of Christians. As such, we owe it to ourselves and to the other members of that community to express and receive the love which Jesus has for each of us, and which he would have us show towards one another in his name.

Penance

For these reasons we should be particularly attentive to the sacrament of reconciliation, or Penance, and especially in the context of the renewed forms for its celebration which the Church provides us with today. This can be an excellent way to celebrate the Easter season, in which we give thanks for Jesus who died and rose again to triumph over sin and death.

Fourth Sunday of Easter

Once more, the initial reading from the New Testament illustrates the preaching of the Good News by Peter (Ac 4:8-12), and the second its articulation in Johannine literature (1 Jn 3:1-2), testifying to the love of God manifest in the person and deeds of Jesus the Christ, who fulfills the Old Testament type of the shepherd (Jn 10:11-18).

Being shut out

The first two readings in today's liturgy both highlight the theme of Jesus, and his followers, being ostracized or ignored. Ostracism, or being shut out and overlooked by those around us, is never easy to take, especially when we feel we are important or we have a significant contribution to make to the very people who seem unreceptive to us and to whatever we have to give.

Various forms of ostracism

Ostracism can take more than one form. In some cases, it can be actively hostile, and this was part of the experience of Jesus and his first followers, as we are well aware from the Biblical narratives and history. This is the kind of rejection which amounted even to physical torture and execution for those who preached the Gospel of Jesus, since their teachings threatened the positions held by some others in power. This form of ostracism, by way of active resistance, is powerful and painful.

Benign neglect

But another form of ostracism is perhaps even more painful, since it is much harder to identify and combat, and that is the tactic of simply ignoring the persons one wishes to shut out. This, too, has happened often enough in the history of Christianity, at the hands of various persecutors throughout the ages. It has even happened *within* the Church, when all-too-human leaders within the Christian community have ignored or shut out certain persons or certain points of view, never really expressing their reasons why, simply because they felt threatened by them. In many instances, later developments have demonstrated that the individuals, groups of people and ways of thought that were shut out for a time or in a particular place or circumstance really had every right to exist and flourish. Some of the saints, including Thomas Aquinas and Joan of Arc, are good examples of this.

Rejecting the cornerstone

And so, ironically enough, we must learn that to be Christian will often mean ostracism because of who we are as Christians or what we hold. It will mean, many times, that what we have to offer may not be seen by others, or may be seen altogether too clearly by those who do not want to see. For this reason, some who would build according to only their own blueprints would reject even the very cornerstone itself.

To come to terms with this kind of reality, of course, is at best painful, and imposes upon us at once a feeling of loneliness. This feeling can easily overtake us, if we forget that—even in what might appear to be ostracism or isolation from the rest, we are indeed members of a community in Christ, and that— as our second reading reminds us today—we are the recipients of the Father's great love, since we are children of God, entitled to a great dignity and personal worth which no man can take away and which no degree of hostility or ostracism can destroy, even when "what we shall later be has not yet come to light."

The price may be high

This will mean, for some of us, laying down our lives as does the good shepherd of the Gospel—not necessarily laying down our lives in the physical sense of martyrdom by execution, as with the earliest Christians (although this is always possible in different circumstances)—but surely at least in terms of recognizing that certain elements of our own personal well-being are less important than our living in the fullest way, as members of Christ's Body in the world which is his Church. This necessarily involves our bearing witness to his Gospel even when that costs us quite a bit personally, for the sake of Christ and the other members of his Body—actual and potential members—whom we are allowed to serve by our own lives. This we do in the name of Christ, making sure to adhere always to his person and his teachings, for as the head of the college of the Apostles tells us, "There is no salvation in anyone else, for there is no other name in the whole world given to men by which we are to be saved."

Fifth Sunday of Easter

The ongoing life of the Church at its earliest stages of growth continues to be narrated through the readings from the Acts, as in our first selection today (Ac 9:26-31). The Church, also, continues its exploration of Johannine passages in the liturgical readings (1 Jn 3:19-24; Jn 15:1-8).

Dignity in Christ's members, but . . .

We learned from the readings of last week's liturgy that if we are adhering conscientiously to the teachings and the person of Jesus, we may expect to be opposed, or even ostracized, to at least some extent. In that light, of course, it is especially necessary for the individual Christian to remember that if he is truly a member in Christ Jesus, he derives his dignity and strength from his very identification with the Lord, and need not be destroyed or intimidated by the ostracism or hostility that may be visited upon him by others. However, the question can easily arise: "How can I have some notion of whether my position is really in line with a Christian identity?" Or put another way, "Can the name of Jesus be used to justify all sorts of—well, aberrations?"

The questions we have just asked are legitimate ones, and honest ones, indeed. After all, it could be quite easy for any individual, with even the most bizarre position or viewpoint, to claim the very authority of the Lord as a defense. In fact, it would appear that this kind of thing is done every day.

We can't "go it alone"

In dealing with or responding to such well-put questions, a key element is to be found in today's Gospel passage, where we are reminded that we are branches of Jesus who is the true vine, and that we must maintain our connection with him in terms of a community structure: the Church. On our own as individuals, operating or attempting to operate in isolation, we can easily go adrift. In that Church which claims to be *Catholic* —which means believing and acting in essential matters as followers of Jesus have done in every time and place—we preserve our authentic connection to the teachings and person of Jesus who is at the center of that mystery we call the Church.

The very nature of being Christian is not to "go it alone," but to live as a member of a body which is the Body of Christ, the Church, with Jesus at its head, and with the type of interdependency between members that is like that of our own human bodies. We, as Christians in the Church, live together in Christ, for otherwise there is no life.

This does not mean to suggest that each of us should be "doormats" in the Church. The various documents of the Second Vatican Council, among other things, would make it clear that we are not only permitted but even obliged to raise questions, express opinions and press for renewal in the Church, all in a spirit of fraternal charity.

The Church as community

There have been those, in recent years, who in good conscience have left the institutional churches, especially the Roman Catholic Church, because of their personal feeling or conviction that within the structure of the Church they could not achieve the changes which they sought in the name of Christ. While it should hardly be our place to judge the motives or personal beliefs of others, we must respectfully and charitably take exception to the point of view they have expressed regarding the institutional Church.

We remain in contact with what Jesus did in his earthly ministry, what he handed down to and through his Apostles, the ways in which they and their successors implemented the teachings of Jesus, not as isolated individuals but as *community*. We partake in the death-and-resurrection of Jesus not as particular individuals but as a sacramental society, becoming further initiated into the mystery of Christ with each celebration of the Eucharist. And we are saved in Christ not as isolated individuals, but as the People of God in the New Covenant. In personal terms, this means for us the opportunity to enjoy the support of the Christian community in times of trial, and even that form of support which is constructive criticism or "feedback." It means, also, the obligation to contribute our own "feedback" into the community at large. This kind of give-and-take is part and parcel of the life of the Church as community and Body of Christ.

Sixth Sunday of Easter

The readings today all relate to the notion of authority as service to others, in first the selection about Peter in Acts (Ac 10:25-26, 34-35, 44-48), then the second reading (1 Jn 4:7-10) which gives us the famous passage "God is love . . .", and finally the Gospel (Jn 15:9-17), which reiterates the Christian notion of authority as stewardship.

Peter's authority

In even the earliest days of Christian history, we can see the authority Peter held in the Church, and the respect he enjoyed from the members of the Christian community. In that light, it is not at all hard for us to envision Cornelius dropping to his knees before Peter. At the same time, we can understand the surprise of Cornelius when Peter shows his discomfort at this type of reverence being shown him. Cornelius, after all, was only doing what he thought was proper in terms of the respect to which he believed Peter was entitled. We can easily sympathize with the position of Cornelius in this situation.

Discarding traditional signs

In recent years, many of us have learned of, or perhaps experienced directly, situations where dignitaries of various kinds, including dignitaries in the Church, have begun to discard some of the traditional signs of respect for their positions. We have seen or heard of or experienced a variety of things which might make us feel uncomfortable.

We have known, perhaps, priests who have wanted people to call them by their first names, instead of "Father." This can be quite a shock to some people. In fact, there are many parents of priests who even call their own *sons* "Father"! Then there are priests who receive the Papal honor of being named a monsignor, but who themselves don't want to be *called* "monsignor." There are bishops today who don't want anyone to genuflect before them to kiss the episcopal ring, and some do not want to be addressed by titles like "Your Excellency." There are a number of priests, prelates and members of religious orders who no longer wish to wear certain types of religious garb or to be addressed by ecclesiastical titles. And when we see this, we might feel uncomfortable, as Cornelius did. How are we to react?

Some flexibility needed

First of all, let it be acknowledged that there are some people who do go to extremes on some of these things, and that what works out well in one person's case may not work out well in another's. We need some healthy room for flexibility and individuality here, so as to serve the needs of a variety of individual persons in the Church as a total Christian community. But, that having been acknowledged, we should see that the priests and brothers and sisters—even some members of the hierarchy —who are taking some of these steps are trying to communicate what Peter said to Cornelius: that they are only human, like their fellow Christians, and that "God shows no partiality." This does not mean that every form of dignity or respect should be done away with. There are some times when these things can be helpful. But they are only means to certain ends, and never ends in themselves. And the end to which these things are means is the end of service, service to the whole People of God and to the world at large in the name of Christ.

Authority is service

And service is the very meaning of authority itself, as Jesus is shown pointing out to his disciples in today's Gospel narrative. His service is one of love, and they are his friends, not his slaves. So, too, with all those who exercise authority in the name of Jesus: they are servants and not masters. It will be hard for some of us to get used to this. And, to be honest, it will even be hard from the standpoint of some who are themselves in positions of authority, and who may have learned about authority and its exercise in some ways which are somewhat at variance from what we understand today—and what Jesus and Peter wanted the first Christians to understand. When this type of difficulty arises, though, we should remember that the officially-designated authorities in the Christian community have no monopoly on the obligation to serve other Christians. Rather, all of us are obliged to serve one another and the total community so as to bring about better understanding and cooperation. ". . . let us love one another, because love is of God . . ."

Seventh Sunday of Easter

Once more in this cycle of liturgical readings, we are given an insight into the life of the early Church (Ac 1:15-17, 20-26). The circumstances of today's passage, the election of Matthias, show how God will not have his People left at a disadvantage by the occurrences of history. This is brought out, too, in the second reading (1 Jn 4:11-16). The Gospel selection (Jn 17: 11-19) presents part of the Fourth Gospel known as the "priestly prayer(s)" of Jesus. In this particular passage, Jesus asks his Father to protect his followers in the world.

Christ's Body will live

The readings for today all illustrate one theme: the Church as the Body of Christ in the world will live, not by virtue of the efforts of men, but precisely because this Body has Christ Jesus at its head. We see in all of the Biblical passages for today's celebration of the Word an assurance that God will abide with his People in the Church of Christ throughout a variety of times and circumstances which might destroy other societies and institutions of human origin.

We have learned in recent years of many prominent churchmen having left the institutional Church for one reason or another, each according to his conscience. Some of these have elected to join other Christian denominations; others have left institutional Christianity altogether. Some of these have not left the Church, but they have been individuals whose particular services to the Church will no longer be forthcoming, since they are no longer in the ranks of priests, religious-order members, active lay leaders, bishops or otherwise active in the life of the Church. And, of course, this is in a way "the tip of the iceberg." These people are *visible* in their ceasing to be active in the life of the institutional Church. What about those who are "below the water line," or far less visible? There are, in addition to lay and clerical leaders and members of religious orders, numerous members of the Church whose activity in the community of Christ has been either terminated or diminished. There are all kinds of reports and statistics to illustrate these trends, and, of course, there are numerous observers who ask whether or not the Church as institution can and will survive.

The Holy Spirit gives the Church life

The answer to that type of question could be found in today's Biblical lessons: the Church will survive not by its own human efforts, but by virtue of its divine origin and sustenance. God who gave life to the Church by sending the Holy Spirit at the first Pentecost will not withdraw that life-giving Spirit.

If the signs of the times are often discouraging today, we might think, what of the loss of one member in the college of the Apostles? Surely, none of the occurrences of our own era could be as much a jolt as that one, at the very outset of Christian history. But the Apostles who remained sought and found another to take his place, and so their ministry continued as it had been envisioned. So it will be with the Church until the end of time. As one or another valuable member leaves the Church—by whatever means, for whatever reason—and as one or another valuable member leaves the Church on earth for the Church in heaven, by virtue of his or her death, the Church will surely survive.

The Church must ask itself questions

Having said this, though, we should not allow ourselves to

become smug, and to assume that the Church's survival gives us cause to dismiss all those who leave the institution. For each one who elects to cease being active in the Church as institution, we should ask ourselves some questions which only a society as secure as the Church can afford to ask: How does the Church as a divinely-founded institution, with human members, fail to live up fully to its divine obligations, thus perhaps frustrating some of its human members out of their roles of activity in the Church? How have I as an individual member of the Church been insensitive to the frustrations or disappointments of another who seeks to serve the Lord in the Christian community? How can the Church more fully be a sign of love in the name of Christ, so that the Church will be more fully a home to all men who hear and love the word of the Lord?

There are those who would object to asking such questions, since they feel that the Church is strong enough to survive without asking them. But the fact is that the Church is even stronger than that: the Church is strong enough to survive— and *thrive*—precisely by asking such questions. And we need have no fear of asking them, since the Lord, we know, will not abandon us.

Ascension

Today's liturgical readings begin with the Acts' account of the ascension of Jesus which begins that book of the life of the apostolic Church (Ac 1:1-11). The idea of Jesus "enthroned" at the right hand of God the Father is carried out in the second reading (Ep 1:17-23). The Gospel (Mk 16:15-20) commands the followers of Jesus to carry on his mission, in the Holy Spirit.

Ascension is not abandonment

The message of Christ's ascension into heaven is not a message of abandonment for the world of men, or for Jesus' followers in the world. On the contrary, it is a message of a fuller and more abiding presence. Following the Ascension, we know, Jesus "seated at the right hand of the Father" symbolizes the acceptance by God the· Father of not only Jesus the Son of God but Jesus the Son of Man. Moreover, and perhaps more to the point right now, Jesus' ascension to the Father paves the way for the sending of the Holy Spirit to give life to Jesus' body in the world which is the Church.

Wisdom needed amid daily confusion

The Holy Spirit, as we are instructed by the Biblical readings for today's liturgy, will have us carry out everything that has been commanded us by the Lord Jesus. To do this, we will need and will receive wisdom. This wisdom will enable us to see clearly, and we will surely be in constant need of it.

The reason why this is so should not be hard to see at all. We are being confused daily; we are being barraged by the hour, it sometimes seems, with contradictory signs and claims and impressions. Through it all, we need clear vision. We are like a navigator who is frustrated by a thick fog or a heavy mist. The object we must see through it all, and which the Spirit will help us to see, can be seen only with "the great hope to which he has called (us)." If there is anything which is confusing or obfuscating to Christians today, certainly it is lack of sufficient hope. We are beset constantly, it often appears, by the prophets of doom, and we are in need of being reminded just as constantly that there is hope and there are bases for hope.

Resurrection—Source of hope

The source of our hope, basically, will be in the fact of Christ's own resurrection, as Paul tells the Ephesians in the pastoral letter read today. If Christ is truly risen, then we have every reason to hope, and to know that in his risen condition —no longer subject to the limitations of time and space in the world—he is truly with us always and everywhere, until even the end of the world. He is truly able to be head of his body in the world, which we know is the Church.

For these reasons we can see salvation and hope in the Lord who died, is risen and will come again. Yet we can wonder, understandably enough, when the fulfillment of the promise of the kingdom will finally come. This is the kind of curiosity shown, legitimately enough, by the apostles as described in today's first reading. And the answer Jesus gives them is for us as well: "The exact time is not yours to know. The Father has reserved that to himself." But we do know that we will be given the assistance we require so that we may be his witnesses ". . . even to the ends of the earth."

Not in isolation

It will be in witnessing to the Lord Jesus, risen and coming again, that we will share with all men "the wealth of (the) glorious heritage to be distributed among the members of the church." And it is precisely because we do *witness* as a church-community that we *worship* together today as a church-community. We witness to the Lord not in one-to-one relationships alone, not in isolation, but precisely as the People of God in the New Covenant, and as members of Christ's body in the world, the Church.

It is in this church-community, too, that we receive in a special way that Holy Spirit who comes to aid us in seeing clearly the message of Easter hope which is in the resurrection and ascension of the Lord Jesus. Here, in the service of the word and the service of the eucharist, we come to know the Risen Christ in a special way, and receive the Spirit he promised to the apostles.

This is the good news of the Lord, which we can then proclaim to all creation. And those of us who are immersed into Jesus' death and resurrection by baptism will be saved. And they, and we, who are baptized in the Lord will continue to bear witness to him and exercise the healing mission which is his in the Church.

Pentecost

The first reading in the liturgy of Pentecost Sunday is the traditional account (Ac 2:1-11) of the upper room's being invaded by the wind (or breath of God) which sends men who had huddled together in fear out into the world in pursuit of those from every land who will listen to the Good News of Jesus; in the latter two readings (1 Cor 12:3-7, 12-13; Jn 20:19-23), the necessity of a Christian's membership in the Spirit is brought out.*

Longevity

The Church celebrates its birthday, we are told, on Pentecost. And when someone celebrates a birthday, we are further told, they have the right to emphasize certain things which might be important to them, especially on that day. Moreover, we know that when someone reaches an advanced age, it is common for the media, in behalf of the general public, to ask them the secret of their obviously long life. So let it be with the Church, on this her birthday. And if it be so, then what will the Church choose to stress by way of observation? What will the Church emphasize as secrets of longevity on her birthday? The answers, as we might well expect, will be found in the

---

*Distinct homiletic suggestions for the Vigil of Pentecost are not made, owing to the diversity of initial Biblical selections that may be chosen for development (*Lectionary*, pp. 131-133).

readings chosen by the Church for this liturgy of Pentecost.

Different forms of ministry

Among the themes of the readings for the Pentecost liturgy will be the most important one stressed in the second reading, from Paul's first letter to the Corinthians. This passage deals with what is coming to be known again in the Church today as diversity or pluriformity of ministry. The language is at once foreign to many of us. The words "ministry" and "minister" do not appear at first to be part and parcel of our Catholic tradition. The nomenclature, instead, is of the sort we commonly associate with "the Protestants." We should remember, at the outset, that the words "ministry" and "minister" come from the Latin word meaning "to serve." Ministry, then, means service, and those who serve are ministers. As a result, the Catholic Church has long identified her servants as ministers. In this way, we have long referred to the bishop or his delegate as the minister of the sacrament of Confirmation, or to the spouses as the ministers of the sacrament of Matrimony, and so on.

It should be clear just from the examples given above that the term "minister" is not the same as "priest." It is true that a priest may be the minister of many of the sacraments, especially the Eucharist. However, others may be the minister of the Eucharist in its distribution, including not only deacons but those whom the Church mandates as extraordinary ministers of the Eucharist (although a priest must celebrate the Eucharistic liturgy and is the ordinary minister of the Sacrament). In addition, there are those who perform ministries which are not directly involved with one or another of the seven sacraments, but which touch upon them. For instance, a minister of the word can be someone who reads the Scriptures at Mass, as a lector; a minister of music can lead the worshipping people of God in expressing their praise in song during the liturgy; a minister of catechesis or religious education can help members of the Church at all ages appreciate their roles in the Body of Christ in the world which is the Church.

There is a tendency to wonder which of these ministries will be of greatest significance or importance in the life of the Church. The Church herself settles the question, again in the same reading from Paul as given in today's liturgy: "There are different ministries but the same Lord; there are different works but the same God who accomplishes all of them in every one. . ." In other words, the different ministries in the Church help one another, and depend on one another, just like the different organs which work together in the same physical body.

All ministries are important

So we see that there are more ordained ministries than just priesthood, and more formal ministries than simply the ordained ones of bishop, priest and deacon. Moreover, if the Church is truly a vital body, it stands to reason that there will be a variety of ministries in the Church which are important and essential even though they might not be in any formal way officially recognized. The person who performs the corporal or spiritual works of mercy—who visits the sick, or who shows other signs of concern, in the name of Christ—is truly exercising the ministry of the Lord and of his Church in a most important and necessary way.

All are involved in ministry

Not long ago a Presbyterian church in New York City, on the front of its building, put up a sign which listed the names of its pastor and associate pastor. And then, when it came to listing the other ministers, the designation was fulfilled simply by mentioning "all members." This concept, in a sense, is an accurate description of Christian ministry. Even though we will have ordained ministers and formal ministries as necessary parts of the Church's structure, we will all be called to Christian ministry which begins with the Lord himself, and in particular to the Catholic tradition, we will exercise, celebrate and reverence all the forms of ministry to which we are called in the name and in the Body of Christ Jesus.

Trinity Sunday

The first reading (Dt 4:32-34, 39-40) *and the second* (Rm 8: 14-17) *compare the giving of the law through Moses in the Old Covenant with the preaching of the apostles after the gift of the Spirit in the New Covenant; in both, it will be difficult for people to accept and adhere to the message, whose import is underscored in the Gospel* (Mt 28:16-20).

For most Catholics, and Christians of all communities, it would be hard to envision a term involving more mystery than the one celebrated in today's liturgy: *trinity.* At once, the word implies both *oneness* and *threeness.*

Three and one

The God of Christians is the One God of Abraham, Isaac and Jacob. We, and our spiritual ancestors the Jews, do not worship the many gods of the pagan peoples who surrounded the Israelites in Egypt. Rather than worship a sun god, a fertility god, a fire god, a water god, we worship only the one Supreme Being who gave the Law to Moses. And in giving the Law to the leader of the People of Israel, this God is described in the book of Exodus as saying "I am Who Am." This can be interpreted as meaning that this God is not to be confused with the functionaries, the gods fashioned by men to do the will of man at every turn. No, this is the One God who is to be adored and not manipulated. This is the God who enters history, indeed *interferes* in man's plans, bringing man to himself and calling attention to his Way, rather than serving the preconceived notions of humanity.

At the same time, the very God who enters human history does so in three persons, whom we Christians recognize as God the Father, the Son and the Holy Spirit. God is one and God is three.

Ways of communicating

Each of these three persons represents a way of communication. The God who communicated with his people in the Old Covenant, who sent his Son to initiate the New Covenant, and who is recognized in the works of creation every day, is called God the Father. When God communicates with us in the ways just mentioned, we humans—trying to find ways of expressing what this communication means—call God a Father. This does not mean that God has a masculine gender, or that God is a father as opposed to the feminine aspect of motherhood. But in human language, the image of life-giver and protector has so often been described by the term "father" that we human beings who try to observe and understand God's care for us call God our father.

The Person who is our salvation in the New Covenant, Jesus the Christ, submits his life to the will of the Father, and we call him the Son of God. All of us are invited to share with Jesus in living in the grace of God, or in divine friendship. All of us are called to be sons and daughters of the one Father. Jesus, who is truly man, is the Son of Man in biblical imagery, and the son of Mary in the flesh. At the same time, Jesus is truly divine and he is the Son of God. (This is why Mary, the mother of Jesus, is given the title "Mother of God.") Jesus is the divine person who makes the One God present "in the flesh."

The same One God is present in the Church, after the final oneness between Jesus, Son of Man and Son of God, with God the Father, which we celebrate in the Ascension of Jesus to God the Father. This presence of God in the Church, and through the

Church in the world, is the product of the unity between the Father and the Son. And since the person who comes in this way gives or breathes life into the world through the Church, we call this person the Holy Spirit.

All One

These persons are three, yet they are all One. When we recognize one of three persons in God as present and acting for the benefit of all men and women, we recognize that all three persons in the same One God are present in this way.

We do well to honor and be aware of the three distinct persons of the Trinity, and to celebrate their saving presence. And when we do so, it is always the same One God that we worship, and whose presence we celebrate, on this Trinity Sunday and every other Sunday.

Assumption (August 15)

The vigil Mass begins with the reading from the first book of Chronicles (1 Ch 15:3-4, 15, 16; 16:1-2), describing the placing of the ark of the covenant in the tent, then proceeds to Paul's triumphant cry over death, conquered by Jesus' resurrection (1 Cor 15:54-57); the Gospel is a brief passage from Luke in praise of Mary (Lk 11:27-28).

In the Mass during the Day, the first reading is from the Apocalypse, or book of Revelation, illustrating Mary as the fulfillment of what the ark meant and stood for (Rv 11:19; 12: 1-6, 10); its second reading, from another segment of First Corinthians (1 Cor 15: 20-26), also illustrates the victory of Christ and his members over death and sin; finally the Gospel (Lk 1: 39-56) recalls Elizabeth's praise of Mary, and her own response is characterized by the Magnificat.

The Assumption and Easter

If we were to think of the Feast of the Assumption of the Blessed Virgin Mary in connection with any other single feast in the liturgical year, which one would it be? Some would immediately answer that this feast of Our Lady should be thought of in relation to another of the Marian feasts. While there is some sense to that, we might look for another connection. That other connection, perhaps subtle yet very simple in a way, is with the central feast of the Christian calendar, Easter.

Easter, of course, is the central celebration of the central

mystery of the Christian faith: as we say in the Acclamation·
during the Eucharistic Prayer or Canon: "Christ has died; Christ
is risen; Christ will come again!"

Sharing in Jesus' triumph

The Assumption of the Blessed Mother clearly celebrates,
in a way, a sharing in Jesus' triumph over death as we know it
in the human condition. For after all, by this dogma of the
Assumption, as carried down through many centuries of Christian
tradition under the Holy Spirit, we know that the fully human
person, like ourselves, who mothered the human person Jesus,
shares especially in one of the chief fruits of his divine power
as Son of God, intended to be shared ultimately by all who believe in him and follow his Way.

Mary is, in a very special way, a sign of the presence of
Christ in the world and among men. At the same time, Mary
in her Assumption is a sign of the union that was obtained between mankind and the Trinity, by virtue of Jesus' rising from
the dead.

At Easter, we celebrate the fact that one true man, also
true God, Jesus, is risen from the dead. The Easter feast suggests
what might be looked for by those who are members of Christ,
in that Body of his which we call the Church. The celebration
of this feast of the Assumption, we could say, "spells it out
more clearly," in its demonstration of one of Jesus' members—
Mary, the very mother and model of the Church—being no
longer subject to death as it had been known until that time.*

---

*Inasmuch as the official teaching of the Church on the
dogma of the Assumption does not specifically state that Mary
died before being assumed bodily into heaven, the above material
does not make specific reference to her death as such, but—
after the *via remotionis* of Aquinas—simply points out that she
did not experience death as we have commonly known it; in a
word, we go no further than does the *magisterium*.

Mary—Church's model and Mother

Mary is the model and mother of the Church for her pro-
tectiveness, her openness to the will of God, and her loyalty
to Jesus the Christ. She is also the first celebrator of Christian
hope and joy.

This should be so, explicitly, in light of our belief that she
was assumed into heaven as her life came to its conclusion.
For by this celebration of Mary's Assumption, we celebrate our
sharing in her hope, her loyalty to the Risen Lord, and her
representing us before the very God to whom we all aspire
to be joined in a way which transcends the limitations of time,
space and the sinful condition of man, which is symbolized by
our common experience of death.

The Assumption is worthy of celebration, then, not only
in its own right, but in a way as a reminder of Easter, which
is that central feast which permeates the celebrations of the
entire Christian liturgical year. Let our faith in the Lord who
is risen, and Mary assumed, permeate our celebration of life in
the very joy and hope that are Mary's, and which should shine
through the life of every Christian.

Second Sunday of the Year

The Old Testament of service to the Lord and to the People of God is illustrated in today's first reading (1 S 3:3-10, 19). The individual Christian's service to God is brought out in terms of avoiding bodily immorality, in the second reading from Paul (1 Cor 6:13-15, 17-20). The Gospel provides the Johannine account of the commission of Peter as Cephas (Rock) to head the Apostles (Jn 1:35-42).

Paul's views on life

Today's second reading, from Paul's first letter to the Corinthians, can be taken in more ways than one. There are some who would like to accuse Paul of being anti-body, anti-women, anti-sex and anti-everything-else. They would use a selection like this as a possible example of their point of view. And when they make such charges, it appears they show how little they understand either of Paul or of Christian tradition concerning earthly life and all its varied dimensions and manifestations.

What Paul is saying—and what the Church has taught over the centuries—is that our life in this world and all of its elements, including most especially bodily human life, is too important to squander. Life—bodily life as we know it—is a great gift of God, to be celebrated for his honor and glory. For this reason, the Church consistently emphasizes the dignity of human life, and this can readily be seen in our own time in regard to a variety of contemporary moral issues having to do with the sanctity of human bodily life.

Sexuality is beautiful

With particular application to the sexual dimensions of human life, the same is true: human sexual encounter—not only bodily, of course, but also in its more important meanings, which are personal, emotional, psychological, spiritual—is too important, too beautiful, too great a gift from God to be wasted, squandered or thrown away.

For this very reason, the Church always has emphasized certain moral principles concerning human sexuality. And because human sexuality is so important and so personal, the Church has always run the risk of being misunderstood—and of contributing to the misunderstanding as well.

Sexual symbols are powerful

The Church has always recognized the communicative power of physical symbols of affection. In fact, the recent rush of sexually-oriented material in print, on the screen and in other media almost seems to suggest that the rest of society is behind the times in catching up with Christians. They, too, now realize the tremendous power of sexual symbols in human life. Unfortunately, though, those who use sexual symbols without considering whether or not these symbols are being used appropriately, meaningfully and responsibly find that the symbols themselves begin to stop *being* symbols, because they cease having meaning. And something very powerful and very meaningful in human life becomes devalued and robbed of its meaning and power.

A balanced view is needed

For so long the Church has taught that we should be careful in our use of sexual symbols of love—not because the Church regards sexuality too little, but precisely because Christians must regard sexuality so highly. And our cause has hardly been helped by those who, in the name of Christ and his Church, have tended to make moral statements which are interpreted in only the most negative way, warning against what people might do *wrong* with their sexual capacities and not stressing enough what people are doing *right* with their sexual capacities. For that particular reason, lots of people—particularly young people —have tended to "turn off" the Church when it comes to matters of sexual morality. In a way, one can understand them. If we had taught as consistently about say honesty in government as we have about honesty in sexual symbols, we might be better off on *both* fronts.

But people seem to be learning that indiscriminate use of sexual symbols can only make something beautiful and massively powerful into something disappointing and destructive in human emotional life, and something no longer conducive to the dignity of the individual Christian person, which sexuality is meant to serve in the first place. Paul put it bluntly: "Every other sin a man commits is outside his own body, but the fornicator sins against his own body. You must know that your body is a temple of the Holy Spirit. . . . So glorify God in your body."

Third Sunday of the Year

The two New Testament readings in the liturgy for today are generally considered as illustrations of the early Christians' expectation of an immediate Second Coming, both in the exhortations of Paul (1 Cor 7:29-31), and in the application some of the first Christians made of Jesus' words as reported in the Gospel (Mk 1:14-20). We see, of course, that the parousia is unpredictable, as the early followers of Jesus came to realize in time. It is perhaps for this reason the Church today provides us with the Old Testament narrative of how the destruction of Nineveh did not come about after all (Jon 3:1-5, 10).

An early Christian view

Biblical scholars generally believe that many first followers of Jesus expected his Second Coming imminently, and only gradually came to realize that perhaps it would not be right away after all. This line of thought appears to be reflected in our second reading today, from Paul's first pastoral letter to the Christian community at Corinth. We today realize that the Second Coming, or "end of the world" is unable to be predicted. But even with that, today's Biblical lessons are not without their applications for us.

The world is passing away

In his message to the Corinthians, Paul tells them, in effect, that the circumstances of their lives should not be taken too seriously, . . . for the world as we know it is passing away." In this context, we can understand some other facets of the early Christian view of things: for example, it was felt that some social abuses, like slavery, should not be challenged or rectified by the Church, since the world as it was would likely be passing away quickly anyway, too quickly for the abolition of slavery in the Roman world to make any difference anyway.

Today we realize that there can easily be a great deal of time between the present moment and the end of time. We realize, too, that the fact of Jesus' incarnation—his becoming flesh and taking unto himself all dimensions of human existence in the world except sin—calls upon us to be no less involved in human life and all its aspects than Jesus himself. At the same time, we can profit from the realization that the world as we know it is not eternal or everlasting. Obviously, this is a paradox: we will be asked to consider two different elements concerning our attitude towards this life.

Two elements in a paradox

One element, which today's Biblical lessons would make clear, is that our lives in this world are transitory, that we need not take too seriously the incidental aspects of everything in our present experience. Instead, we should take the long-range view, reacting to things in terms of how they fit into the eternal scheme of salvation. For this reason, we are well aware as Christians, we should not place undue emphasis on material wealth, fame, and other aspects of this life which can be so fleeting.

We are never excused from social responsibility

But that does not excuse us in any way from an obligation to take with the greatest seriousness those matters which relate directly to the values of the Gospel: love, justice, brotherhood, peace among men. And the Church has realized, with every instance in the social order, that questions of economic injustice, racial bigotry, international relations, war and peace are very much the business of each and every one of us who would take seriously our identity as a member of Christ's Body in the world, the Church, and our understanding that Jesus, the Word of God, was made flesh.

One way to put these different elements into proper perspective is to consider whether something is important only to us, or to man, on a larger scale. Is this or that particular concern important because it means something to *me*, in a selfish or limited way, or is it important in the total scheme of things for its possible effect on mankind generally, and because of its power to demonstrate the glory and love and justice of God, the Father, Son and Holy Spirit? If we ask ourselves questions like this honestly, with a sense of balance and fairness, we will be likely to come to some appreciation of what our priorities in life should be. And in doing this and acting accordingly, we can be sharers in the saving incarnation of Jesus the Son of God, and in the becoming-flesh of the very Word of God in the world.

Fourth Sunday of the Year

The first reading illustrates the fact that Law will be followed by prophecy in the Old Testament, as a reminder to Israel of their identity and obligations as the Chosen People of the Covenant (Dt 18:15-20). The second selection, taken out of context, has been used as "evidence" of an anti-sexual bias on Paul's part, and as an argument for mandatory celibacy among the clergy, although the Church universal has never recognized it as such (1 Cor 7:32-35). The final passage from the Gospel (Mk 1:21-28) illustrates Jesus' power over even devils, as another sign of his divine mission.

Marriage and celibacy

The selection we read today from St. Paul's first pastoral letter to the Christians at Corinth could lead to a great deal of misunderstanding in the Christian community today. There are those who would be quick to read into this passage a downgrading of the married state, or an unfavorable comparison of it to celibacy. This type of analysis usually leads to the erroneous conclusion that the Church cannot have any married persons exercising its ministry. However, we know that in Paul's time married persons did indeed exercise various ministries in the Church, including even the highest offices in the college of Bishops. Even in later centuries, the Church has admitted legitimately married Bishops and Popes, as well as priests, deacons and other ministers. Even today, married members of the Christian community serve as extraordinary ministers of the Eucharist, deacons and, in some circumstances, as priests.

So what Paul is saying here is not in any way a command, just an opinion based on his own personal reflections. Studies of the New Testament, also, indicate that Paul is possibly reflecting an attitude we saw in the previous week's Biblical lesson from the same first Epistle to the Corinthians: the earliest Christians tended to believe that the Second Coming of Jesus was immediate, and that they would do well to leave their states of life unaltered and uncomplicated as much as possible (the single remaining single and not marrying) so as to devote all their time and energies to preparing for this imminent return of the Lord in full glory.

Celibacy is a sign

Today, the Church still realizes a value to celibacy or virginity in the priesthood and in religious-order life, as a sign of the world that is to come—the theologians, in their language, would call this "eschatological witness." The idea behind this is that even the wonderful Sacrament of Matrimony which God gives us for the living-out of our lives in this world is not for everyone, and that even this Sacrament may be foregone by those who wish to emphasize in a most dramatic way their focus on relationships which are broader in time and place than those of marriage and family life. For this reason, we do well to always honor the tradition of celibacy, whether in the priesthood, or in religious-order life, or in the consciously chosen witness of lay persons in the Church. There have been those, in various times and places, who have sought to downgrade or make light of this witness, and they have been short-sighted and have missed the point.

Marriage must be honored

At the same time, we cannot honor celibacy without honoring marriage. For this reason, we should always hold the Sacrament of Matrimony in the highest esteem. And one way of doing this is to embrace joyously and with complete respect and gratitude those married ministers the Church gives to us, whether they be ministers of music, or extraordinary ministers of the Eucharist, or deacons, or—in the circumstances where this applies—priests.*

There are some individuals in the Church, unfortunately, who are slow to see this—the ones who would prefer to receive Holy Communion from a celibate priest or deacon rather than a married deacon or extraordinary minister of the Eucharist. These people do no honor to celibacy, whether or not they think they do. They also do no honor to marriage (including, if they are married, their own married lives). Furthermore, they do no honor to the Eucharist, which is the presence of Christ in the Church and the sign of the unity of the entire Church in all its members and all their states of life. For all our ministers, married and celibate, let us truly thank the Lord who gives them to us as his people.

---

*This reference may be confusing in the average American Catholic community, but it should be remembered that married priests function not only in the Uniate oriental rites, but in a limited number of circumstances in the Western Church as well, and where this exists with the legitimate sanction of Church authority, it should be respected and not dismissed as an oddity.

Fifth Sunday of the Year

The Old Testament sapiential literature provides us with the first reading (Jb 7: 1-4, 6-7), describing the frustration of man's lot in earthly life, to which the Gospel provides the answer in the power of Jesus (Mk 1:29-39). The Epistle reading from Paul (1 Cor 9:16-19, 22-23) underscores the obligation to proclaim the Gospel message.

The first reading today is from the portion of the Old Testament known as the "sapiential" or "wisdom" literature, in that these passages reflect the religious wisdom of their time, several centuries before the time of Christ. In the well-known Book of Job, we are given today one of many selections in which the person of Job expresses on behalf of mankind in general a number of the frustrations which every one of us must find and face from time to time in life.

A "spinning joke"

Sometimes, life does seem a vicious cycle indeed. In his verse-play adaptation of the Book of Job, entitled *J.B.,* Archibald MacLeish has one of his characters express the notion that life is a "spinning joke" with man as its victim. There is little encouragement to be found in that type of expression, but every one of us perhaps feels like that from time to time.

Life can indeed seem a drudgery when we find ourselves doing the same things, day in and day out, in the same old way.

For this reason we often find that things are repetitious to the point of monotony. How do we survive in the face of it all? Of course, with a proper Christian perspective on life, we realize that the world is made new by God every day, with new and ever more glorious manifestations of God's love and providence for us. But sometimes even this cannot be seen clearly by those of us whose senses and appreciations for even the divine may be dulled by the boredom of day-to-day living and everyday running on the proverbial treadmill.

Dr. Peter's prescription

Dr. Laurence J. Peter, who wrote the famous book *The Peter Principle: Why Things Always Go Wrong*, wrote a sequel to it not long ago called *The Peter Prescription*, on how to make things go right. One of the things Dr. Peter suggests among his "pre-scriptions" is that each of us should "take a vacation every day." We may be used to the travel posters on the commuter train or bus, luring us away from the workaday world to some exotic place. And we may notice in flipping from the sports to the financial to the want-ad pages of our daily newspaper, a number of advertisements inviting us to take a plane, boat or train to someplace else where we can "get away from it all." But most of us can't afford the time and money to do this with great fre-quency: for average people, a vacation once every year or two is about all that they can manage.

A vacation can be every day

But when Dr. Peter prescribes "a vacation every day" he does not refer to a physical relocation or the laying-out of a great deal of time or money. He simply means that each of us should find those things we most enjoy that can be done on a daily basis, and take the time to do them as part of our daily routine. It may be a walk after dinner in the evening, or a leisurely second cup of coffee in the morning, or a few moments' conversation with a valued friend, or a few moments alone thinking and relaxing. But whatever it is, if it can be done daily without great hardship to others, and if it helps us to see the newness of each day, Dr. Peter prescribes that we do it.

A "mini-retreat"

In our own spiritual lives, there is room for the same principle: take some time every day, however little we might be able to afford, to retreat from the world and contemplate our position as members of the community of Christ, sharers in his saving death and resurrection. We can see what this means to us and what our perspective on life should be as a result. This word "retreat" as it was just used often conjures up the image of going away to some place, perhaps for a weekend or even longer, as has often been done by many in search of a fuller spiritual life. We realize, though, that is something that often cannot be done. What we are proposing here, though, is a sort of "mini-retreat," a little "break" every day, that may give us a chance to get back into tune with ourselves, our lives, their meanings, and the God who is the source and author of it all. In that way, we need not feel so much under the dead weight of monotony, or so helplessly tied to the treadmill. We will then be in a position to echo the words of today's responsorial psalm: "Praise the Lord, for he is good; sing praise to our God, for he is gracious; it is fitting to praise him."

Sixth Sunday of the Year

Both the first and last readings today focus on the theme of healing as a sign of God's presence, in first the priestly function of healing in the Old Testament, as with Aaron (Lv 13:1-2, 44-46) and then the healing ministry of Jesus in the New Testament (Mk 1:40-45). The Epistle selection (1 Cor 10:31-11:1) is so brief that it requires explanation in context: the Jewish and Gentile (Greek) Christians, having different senses of obligation (i.e., the Mosaic Law) were in danger of offending one another, even unwittingly; Paul reminds them that the righteousness of their own positions in conscience does not allow them to be careless about the sensitivities of others.

Jews and "Greeks"

In the early Church, there were those Jews who embraced Jesus and his Gospel, seeing therein the fulfillment of all they had learned in the Law and the Prophets, as the coming of the Messiah. It seemed only natural to them that their worship of Jesus should combine with their continued observance of the Mosaic Law in all its specific dimensions, including such things as dietary laws for what could or could not be eaten or drunk, and under what circumstances. Those who accepted Jesus who were *not* Jews—the ones the New Testament frequently calls the "Greeks"—were not obliged to follow the Mosaic Law. In fact, at the Apostles' gathering—later considered the first Council in the Church—at Jerusalem, it was decided after quite some discussion that these Gentiles or "Greeks" did not need to take onto themselves the obligations of the Mosaic Law, did not need to become Jews, in effect, in order to become Christians. That Council at Jerusalem should have settled the question once and for all. But, just as there are members of the Church who still do not understand what was taught by our own most recent Council in our own time, there were those —especially in an age of limited communications—who failed to understand what the teaching of the Apostles was at the Council of Jerusalem. So it became necessary for Paul in his pastoral letters to remind the members of the Church in various places of what the Apostles and the Holy Spirit had decided, and how this teaching was to be put into practice in daily Christian life.

Mutual respect

In the passage we read today from Paul's first letter to the Corinthians, we see the Apostle trying to ensure good relations between Jews and "Greeks." He wants each to respect the position of the other, all the while realizing that they are perfectly right in following their own particular tradition as a matter of obligation in conscience. This meant that while it might have been all right for the Gentiles or "Greeks" to eat certain things or drink certain things in this circumstance or that manner, it was not all right for them to do so in a way that might give unnecessary offense to the Jews who were their neighbors. The rightness of one's own position in conscience is never a license to offend others unnecessarily, and this is what Paul attempts to point out in this Epistle.

Diverse Christian approaches

We live in a time when we are coming to appreciate the diversity of approaches to Christian life, both among different Christian denominations and even within the Roman Catholic Church itself—sometimes according to different rites, often within the same Roman Rite but according to different practices, dispensations, national hierarchies, localities or other categories. We are in a good position to realize that there is a need for each one of us to respect our own position and our own traditions, all the while not downgrading or failing to appreciate the position and traditions of others.

A lesson worth remembering

It is very easy, of course, since we understand the reasons behind our own position or traditions, to give short shrift to those of others'. We can derive a certain amount of satisfaction from envisioning our own way of looking at and doing things as being more fully in keeping with the traditions of the Church than even our very neighbors within the Church. There are times, of course, when Church authority will have legitimate reason to spell out what is required or what is prohibited by the essentials of the Gospel message entrusted to the Church as community of faith. But beyond that, even when pursuing and defending our own ways of living the Christian life, we have no call to make light of others'. This is the lesson Paul taught to the Corinthians and to the other Christian communities of the time in which he served (the Galatians and the Romans, for instance) and all for the sake of preserving the necessary unity of the Church. In our own time and circumstances, it is still a lesson learned with difficulty, and worth remembering.

Seventh Sunday of the Year

The readings today present us with two images of reconciliation and healing, first in the Old Testament (Is 43:18-19, 21-22, 24-25), then in the Gospel (Mk 2:1-12). The Epistle (2 Cor 1:18-22) illustrates the consistency of the Lord who saves, heals and forgives through Christ Jesus.

Avoiding misunderstanding

Last week we concentrated on a selection from Paul's first Epistle to the Corinthians, where we saw that the Jews who embraced Jesus and his Gospel, and also the non-Jews or "Greeks," as they were called, in the early Church, had reason to respect both their own different traditions and those of each other. We saw, in applying this lesson to our own time and circumstances, that we here and now have reason to respect our own traditions and practices and points of view, but at the same time to respect those of others, both within the Roman Catholic community, and also among other denominations within Christianity.

Even in the first regard, our fellows in the same denomination, there is likely to be occasional difficulty or misunderstanding, because of the difference of tradition between rites, nationalities, or geographic regions. But in terms of relationships with other Christian denominations—in the context of what has commonly been known as "the ecumenical movement," the difficulties appear to multiply.

We should acknowledge, right away, the fact that the authority of our Church will move to keep us from engaging in things that would be excessive or premature, even in an atmosphere which might be quite optimistic at times for further cooperation and communication between Christian bodies. But even with safeguards like that, even with a sufficient degree of necessary caution, there is a tendency to approach dialogue with other Christians with an attitude of fear, suspicion, and even resentment. Attitudes like this are in one sense horrible and lamentable, since they contradict Jesus' priestly prayer that we all be one in his name. But, at the same time, if we are to be honest with ourselves as human beings, then perhaps we should admit that these attitudes are quite understandable.

Interdenominational crossfire

Any history of Christianity, written from practically any viewpoint, will show injustices, insensitivities, atrocities and insults from Catholic to Protestant, from Protestant to Catholic, Uniate to Orthodox, Orthodox to Uniate, in what seems almost a continual interdenominational crossfire over many centuries. The fact that, in recent years, we have come as far as we have in building bridges in the direction of reconciliation is in itself a sure sign of the presence of the Holy Spirit in our midst. But even with that hopeful sign, most of us will remember the "horror stories" that have been impressed upon us very early in life, and often repeatedly, which tell us why we really should not trust one another. At its worst extreme, this kind of thing shows itself in the interdenominational strife of a place like Ireland, where people kill each other in the name of Christ— or so they would think—even when the really religious aspects of the division have been long forgotten, and only the unfortunate atmosphere of mistrust lingers. In its less extreme forms, this kind of attitude can be seen among the Catholics— and Protestants—who may engage in this or that ecumenical service at the appointed time, like during the Church Unity Octave, but who are generally reluctant to enter into conversation with Christians of other denominations. There is, after all, such a history of hostility between us.

The past is the past

If we are to get anywhere, we must realize that the past is the past indeed. And this is just what is set down for us in today's first Biblical text from the prophetic book of Isaiah. The Lord asks us not to remember the events of the past, because he is capable of wiping out our offenses. This means the offenses of all of us, both those who have offended us and also those of us who have offended others. This the Lord does in the name of Jesus, whom our Gospel today presents as healing by way of forgiveness and reconciliation. In the name of the same Jesus, to whom all Christians bear witness, let us take full advantage of his healing love which reconciles us one to another. This means approaching one another not in mistrust or suspicion or fear, which we have done for all too many years now, but rather with real openness to one another and to God's grace. This we can do precisely because we believe what has been told us by our first reading today, that God is doing something new for us.

Eighth Sunday of the Year

In today's Old Testament passage we get a glimpse of the image of Yahweh as the constant bridegroom and Israel as the fickle and adulterous bride, after the manner of the prophet Hosea and his own wife Gomer (Ho 2:16-17, 21-22). In the Epistle (2 Cor 3:1-6), Paul demonstrates that the acceptance of his preaching by the community stands as evidence of its legitimacy. The Gospel shows Jesus' insistence on renewal of spirit, in terms of preparedness for the new kingdom that is to come.

In recent weeks we have focused on one important aspect of our Scriptural readings: the need to understand and respect the viewpoints and traditions of others who worship the same Lord and God, sometimes in different ways in the same denomination, and sometimes in different denominations as well, and we have observed both the difficulties presented by life and human history, and also the grace and help provided by God, in doing this.

Reconciliation

Today, we see an interesting image of reconciliation, taken from the Old Testament book of the prophet Hosea. Hosea, himself the husband of an unfaithful wife, attempted to bring her back to him. It is not hard for us to envision how difficult it was for him to do this, employing a necessary mixture of firmness and tenderness. The prophets of the Old Testament frequently communicated the Word of God to Israel in terms of their own human experiences and surroundings (for example, Amos was a shepherd, and frequently used images pertaining to sheep and shepherds). Accordingly, Hosea's book of prophecy will present the image of God as the faithful and loving husband, who must chastize and bring back to himself Israel the unfaithful bride, combining firmness with tenderness, in ways which we have seen in various aspects of Salvation-History.

Reminders of identity

In the present day, we can see how we Christians, both in our individual lives and in our community life as a Church, have often been unfaithful to the New Covenant, much as Israel was unfaithful to the Old. Again, God combines tenderness and firmness in bringing us back to him by his grace, in the person of our Lord Jesus. And, just as with Israel of old, it will become necessary at times to remind us of our identity and obligations in covenant by way of some prophetic utterance or communication.

We have been unfaithful

In our own times, the prophets have told us that, sometimes even despite our best efforts, we have not been fully true to ourselves as a Church, or to the Lord as his community of faith and practice in the world. This is so because we have become somewhat bogged down in certain patterns of thought or action, or sometimes inaction. We have tended at times to fall astray from the word of God, and to take on too much the particular trappings of this or that time or culture in history. To the extent that we may have done this, we need to be called back. Sometimes this can be done with great tenderness and compassion by those prophets who function as God's messengers in the Church, and sometimes it is done harshly. It is a difficult situation for striking a balance. Lack of sufficient firmness may cause the message to go unheeded. Excessive bluntness may make the messenger or his message offensive to the ears of men, and so the essentials of the message are in danger of going unheard.

Careful evaluation

But we should pay as much attention as we can to these utterances, evaluating them carefully whenever possible. We should pay attention not simply to the manner of their presentation—for this or that particular style of communication may at times prove to be misleading or deceptive—but rather, we should concentrate to whatever extent we possibly can upon the *substance* of the message that is being communicated to us in such a way as to call us back to be more truly and more fully what we are called to be in and by Christ.

This kind of attention to our own faults and failings and shortcomings, either as individual Christians or as a total Church community—can sometimes be a frustrating process, and can cause us at times to feel that we are being called upon to forsake our very identity, or to become less authentically Catholic in some kind of reform or another. In such situations, we do well to rely on reputable spokesmen of the Church itself, who can weigh these things against the Biblical, traditional and historical evidences for what the Church truly should be and asks us to be. In this way, to refer to the imagery of today's Gospel, we will find new wine being put into skins that are prepared properly.

Ninth Sunday of the Year

The first reading, from Deuteronomy (Dt 5:12-15), illustrates the Mosaic Law of Sabbath, which is interpreted in the context of the New Covenant in the Gospel selection (Mk 2:23-28). In the second reading of today's liturgy, Paul returns to an image highlighted several times in recent liturgical passages: the shining of divine light even in what often appears as darkness (2 Cor 4: 6-11).

Today's readings from Sacred Scripture emphasize both the nature of the Sabbath obligations, and also the need to regard these with a certain degree of maturity and flexibility, all the while being neither too easy nor too hard on ourselves, as with other obligations.

The purpose of Sabbath

The whole purpose of Sabbath, or of keeping the Lord's day holy, is that we remain mindful of our obligations to the Lord in the first instance. Whatever might be our lot in life, our responsibilities in the world, or our situation in life, we are called upon to draw back from all of that, once a week at least, to remember who we are in the most basic way, and what our ultimate identity and destiny must be as creatures of God, owing him reverence.

In the Mosaic Law of the Jews, which has been adapted for use by the followers of Jesus in the New Covenant, the Sabbath obligation has two aspects. The first of these is to spend the

day in worship of the Lord our God. The second is to achieve
that end, in part, by refraining from work.

Flexibility

In recent years, we have come to regard those obligations
flexibly, just as Christians changed the Sabbath from the Jewish
observance of Saturday to the observance of Sunday, the Lord's
Day, when the Resurrection took place, according to Christian
tradition.

The worship of our Lord, once a week at least, can now take
place by way of anticipation or transferred observance, rather
than merely on Sunday. When the Church decided this, she did
so in the same spirit that prevailed when the Lord's Day, for
Christians, first became Sunday rather than Saturday.

Work is complex

The obligation to refrain from work has been interpreted
more flexibly than before, by necessity, largely for the same
reason that called for the more flexible interpretation of the
first obligation, namely worship. No longer do we live in a
sort of society where all work can stop on a given day. Some
of us—policemen, doctors, nurses, firemen, service station attend-
ants—are obliged to serve the community according to need,
regardless of the day or the hour.

Moreover, there is even room for some flexible interpretation
as to just what constitutes work in an individual's life. For
some people, playing baseball is fun. For a professional athlete,
it may be work and fun. Manual labor may be gainful employment for some people. For others, it may be a release from the
pressures of a job which requires mental, not physical, effort.
In any case, the principle is this: that when we can—preferably
on the Lord's Day, but at least every week if we can—we take
time out from whatever it is we would normally do, and engage
in some rest and relaxation, and some *reflection*, that would
give us an opportunity to see the light of God shining through

the circumstances and obligations and routines of our daily lives, as an outgrowth of that light which he gives us in the liturgy of the community gathered together to worship him.

"Change of pace"

The ways in which we do this may well vary from individual to individual, or from family to family. That is well and good . . . but the important thing is that in some fashion or another, we do it, we take a "break" from the everyday activities of our lives, and allow a "change of pace" so that we may come to remember who we are and where we are going, and how we will be who we are and go where we are going only with the light that is Christ.

Tenth Sunday of the Year

The first reading (Gn 3:9-15) provides us the story of Adam caught in his defiance of the Lord's command, and banished from paradise. This legend illustrates the fact of man's separation from God at the outset of human experience in the world. The second reading contrasts Adam in the old order with Jesus as the New Adam, the one in whom all will enjoy a new relationship with God the Father (2 Cor 4:13-5:1). The Gospel shows how Jesus has power even over the devils (Mk 3:20-35).

God versus Satan

In our Gospel narrative today, we see Jesus demonstrating the basic opposition between God and Satan, in response to a question as to where he and his followers should be counted. Over the past few years, we have seen an increased interest in the person and power of Satan, in books, movies and other phenomena of our popular culture. In that regard, too, the basic opposition is illustrated, in that those who do not consider themselves very religious, when they assert the belief that there exists a demonic power, argue in effect for the opposite as well: the power of God which does battle with evil.

To some, the devil emerges as more of a figurative image than a reality. This is the implication suggested by Father John Reedy, not so long ago, in *A.D. Correspondence,* to the effect that Satan's figure is sought out by man attempting to explain evil among men and particularly as it may be found within oneself.

The devil is real enough

But there is a growing number of people for whom the devil is real enough, indeed. Included in this number are the people flocking to see movies or plays, or buy books, about Satan, possession, and various forms of occult worship and ritual, as we have seen in our society over the past several years.

To some, including Father Richard J. Woods, at Loyola University, this has amounted to more than a mere fad. For some, Father Woods suggested in *The National Catholic Reporter* a while back, occultism is a revolt against modern technocracy. For others, it is a reaction against what they see as Christianity's failure to respond meaningfully to the problems posed by that technocracy.

Need for the transcendent

Woods has analyzed the current interest in Satanism and the occult as a symptom of man's need for a deeper, more perceptible experience of the transcendent in human life. It would be ironic, indeed, if Christianity, in attempting to streamline sacramental life and devotion, were to unwittingly steer people in the direction of bizarre rituals which themselves would be directly opposed to the Person and the Gospel of Jesus Christ.

Serious business

The evidence concerning the recent wave of interest in the occult is probably not all in yet, but enough of it is to suggest that—at least in large measure—this is serious business, and not to be laughed off or taken lightly. The Church—we—can respond to this phenomenon, and perhaps others like it, by seeking an ever-increasing variety of ways in which to draw attention to and focus upon the mysteries of the Christian sacramental life, and the saving presence of the Lord Jesus in the Church—particularly in the sacrament of the Holy Eucharist, at once remembering all that is essential to that life and all that may be done to engender its growth in an age of culture shock and future shock.

As Paul says to the Corinthians: "We do not lose heart because our inner being is renewed each day. . . . The present burden of our trial is light enough and earns for us an eternal weight of glory beyond all comparison. We do not fix our gaze on what is seen but on what is unseen. . . ."

Meet evil with faith

With faith in the Father, the Son and the Holy Spirit, let us renew our attention to their presence in our lives, and draw upon the strength of that presence in dealing with the evil dimensions of the human condition which we experience.

The above is essentially based on an editorial entitled "Deviltry," from *The Advocate* (Archdiocese of Newark, N.J.), November 1, 1973, and is reprinted here with permission.

Eleventh Sunday of the Year

The first reading, from the Old Testament book of the prophet Ezekiel, affords us an image of an Israel whose source will be small and unimpressive in itself (Ez 17: 22-24). This will be important in terms of the visions Ezekiel presents of a restored Israel after the Babylonian Exile. The importance of the after-life in the resurrection over the earthly life in the body is the subject of the second reading from Paul's second pastoral letter to the Christian community in the Church at Corinth (2 Cor 5:6-10). In the passage from the Gospel according to Mark (Mk 4:26-34), we see the famous story of the mustard seed, another way of bringing home the same lesson as that exposed in the initial reading in this liturgy.

Great from small

"Great things have small beginnings" could be the theme of today's celebration of the Word of God in Sacred Scripture. We see this brought out in a familiar way in the Gospel story of the mustard seed, in a less familiar way, perhaps for some of us, too, in the Old Testament reading from the prophet, Ezekiel, concerning the renewal of Israel after her exile into Babylon. In both readings, the message is clear: the kingdom of God will have humble origins. It is important to remember this whenever we tend to think too much of religion in terms of statistics, attendance figures, real estate, buildings, attitudinal survey analyses, membership charts and financial reports. This is not to say that such factors are utterly without meaning. But their value must be put into proportion, or else we will misread "the signs of the times."

Not long ago, in a major Catholic university, a sociology professor did a survey on the effect of Catholic education as compared with public school, from the elementary through collegiate levels. His norm for measurement, or the "religiosity factors" he used, were statistics of religious observance: frequency of attendance at Mass, frequency of the Sacraments, and so on. One could hardly debate the value of the sacramental life for a Catholic. However, it would seem superficial to use those factors alone in attempting to determine whether or not someone is genuinely religious. Indeed, later such studies have added questions concerning religious and moral *attitudes*, and ways in which these might be translated into everyday Christian life.

Externals can mislead

So, those of us who tend to be impressed, positively or negatively, with the buildings and property the Church owns, or the number of its members, or other such phenomena, should remember that these things are only externals. The externals, of course, represent to some extent the inner life of the community, but they are not *themselves* the inner life of the community, nor are they any substitute for it.

It was important for the first Christians to realize this, so small was their number, so few were their earthly signs of presence, and so powerful did their opponents appear. It is important for us to remember, too, especially in an era when the pundits are interpreting every statistic, upward and downward, concerning Church membership and attendance, ratio of priests and religious order members to laity, enrollment figures in Catholic schools, financial conditions in this or that diocese, and so on. This does not mean, of course, that we should not hope for healthy membership in the Church, and for devotion to the Mass and the other sacraments, or for vigorous religious and priestly lives, or fiscal solvency, or quality Catholic education.

But it does mean that "the numbers game" simply cannot, and never could, "tell the whole story."

Christianity itself began with small numbers, as did the remnant of Israel which Ezekiel envisions in his prophecies. So have a number of great and praiseworthy causes and apostolates in the history of the Church. Even today, some of the greatest gifts of the Spirit in the life of the Church (the work of certain missionary groups, for instance) must be measured in other than numerical terms.

Balanced view

The application of this lesson, surely, is twofold. On the one hand, we have no cause for overconfidence, smugness or complacency whenever it is mentioned that this or that statistic concerning the life of the Church appears to be of immensely impressive magnitude. At the same time, especially in a period of change in the life of the Church and the lives of its members individually, we have no cause for despair or panic when it appears that this or that aspect of Church activity is less formidable or favorable, numerically or statistically, than it was before.

There will be examples, in Scriptural narratives, of large numbers—for instance, the crowds that were fed by Jesus, both with food and by his Word, or those who heard Peter after the Holy Spirit had given life to the infant Church. But in the upper room, or at Calvary, and so many other places that are important in the history of Christ's presence in the world before and after Pentecost, there were only a few.

Twelfth Sunday of the Year

In the Old Testament book of Job, the sapiential legend has God responding to the anguished inquiries of Job by stressing his pre-existent dominion (Jb 38:1, 8-11). The freedom of those who have died in Christ from the life of the world as we have known it is the theme of Paul's second pastoral letter to the Corinthians (2 Cor 5:14-17). These two themes combine in the Gospel story of Jesus calming the seas and the winds (Mk 4:35-41).

God's dominion

The image of God which the Scriptures present to us today is overwhelmingly an image of the Lord God Jehovah, the Almighty One, who is over all and in all, and who has dominion over all the universe. In our first reading for the liturgy today, we are put into the context of the Book of Job, in the sapiential or wisdom literature of the Old Testament. Job, having been beset by a series of plagues and trials, asks God why this should be so, in light of the good life Job has lived. In responding, God is depicted as telling Job, in effect, that he need not be accountable to a mortal creature, for his is power and authority over all. The dialogue between Job and God, of course, is a story meant to illustrate several points. And one point that comes through in this reading, as well as the other two for today, is that not only the Lord, but those who put their faith and trust in him, will be freed from the limitations of life in the world as we know it. This will be so for Christians, Paul tells the Corinthians, because of our sharing in the resurrection of Jesus, "... so that those who live might live no longer for themselves, but for him who for their sakes died and was raised up. . . . This means that if anyone is in Christ, he is a new creation. The old order has passed away; now all is new!"

The power of the Lord is brought out, too, in the rather graphic narrative of the Gospel according to Mark, where elements which man has always tended to be in awe of—wind and the sea—are seen as subject to the Lord Jesus, and this for the benefit of those who will believe in him. This type of imagery is part of man's religious heritage throughout the centuries, in various cultures, and helps illustrate the power of the deity.

The Lord is above all

In both the first reading and the Gospel of today's series of liturgical passages from Scripture, we see the same kind of description: the Lord is above all the forces of nature, which he has in fact created. And if primitive man in his earliest expressions of religious faith tended to look towards divine power as manifest in such forces as the sea or the wind, how much more would man later come to appreciate the power of the Creator in the Judaeo-Christian tradition? Unlike the adherents of some primitive pagan religions, we see God as not only the master of nature, or the custodian of the forces of the *cosmos*, but as the One having dominion over all, as Almighty Lord.

This type of power is expressed in our liturgical expressions of faith: "Holy, Holy, Holy Lord, God of power and might. Heaven and earth are filled with your glory. . . ." And the power we recognize in God the Father, we recognize in his Son Jesus, as in our reading from the Gospel according to Mark today. The power and lordship we see in Father and Son, we see too in the Holy Spirit, who gives life to the Body of Christ in the world, which is the Church.

We act in the Spirit

There is a danger of confusion here, in that we might tend

to see God's power as some sort of excuse for our own inactivity.
One inference we could draw from today's readings, particularly
the one from the Old Testament book of Job, is that our own
actions or deeds are virtually insignificant in comparison with
those of God and that, therefore, we ought to do nothing. There
are people, we know, who tend to feel that since God is all-
powerful, man should sit back and take whatever comes from
God. If we feel this way, we tend to forget something just made
clear to us, and worth stressing with great vigor: the all-powerful
God is present in his Son Jesus, who in turn is present in his
Body the Church, and we are the members of that Body of Christ
in the world, given life by the Holy Spirit. This means that there
is not only no excuse for passivity on our part, but that there is,
instead, every reason for activity which is enlightened and given
life by the Spirit.

Basis in faith

Those of us who are, in fact, sharers in the resurrection of
the Lord Jesus, and members of his Body, the Church, have
good reason to act as his Body in the world, confident that we
will be given life and sustained by the Holy Spirit, as a sign
of the overwhelming power of God that we acknowledge in faith.
And when we tend to feel that the forces of frustration and
evil are perhaps closing in on our own efforts and all seems hope-
less, then we can turn to the words of today's Gospel, "Why
are you so terrified? Why are you lacking in faith?"

Thirteenth Sunday of the Year

The Old Testament reading from the book of Wisdom (Ws 1: 13-15; 2:23-24) shows how God, as author of life, can hardly rejoice in death; however, man, by his initial rejection of divine friendship, brings upon himself death as we know it. Jesus, however, is capable of healing the human condition, even in its sickness and death, as shown in the Gospel (Mk 5:21-43) and second selection (2 Cor 8:7-9, 13-15) for today's liturgy.

God does not want suffering

Whatever we need, and ask for through the Lord and in his name, we should ask for with confidence, in the grace of Jesus the Risen Christ. If this seems a presumption, or a bold stance to take, we are advised in our first reading today, from the sapiential (wisdom) literature of the Old Testament, that God wants us not to suffer, but does all in our favor. Therefore, as our Gospel selection is quick to point out, we should ask God in faith and hope to be attendant to our needs.

There are, though, a couple of things worth remembering in this context, lest we misunderstand.

We will receive the Spirit

The first of these is that we will not always receive exactly what it is that we seek to begin with. What we *will* receive, Jesus guarantees us in the New Testament, is the Holy Spirit. The Holy Spirit, the Advocate, will enlighten our minds and wills and hearts so as to help us see our priorities in light of Jesus and his Gospel. This will mean, on some occasions, that we will have to reconsider or realign our priorities ... to ask ourselves, "Do I really want this?" or "Is this really best for me and all others concerned?" Sometimes the answer will be yes; sometimes we call on the Advocate to help us see that the answer will have to be *no*, and the good we originally sought will be replaced, in effect, by an even greater good.

No competition

The second thing to remember is that we are not in competition with others for either the attention or the providence of God. So often, we have experienced or heard of situations where a parent, a teacher, or some other person must divide his or her attention and energies, and is unable to devote all at once to one person or subject. Because we tend to measure things in terms of our human experience, we are tempted to do the same with the Lord, and therefore to feel that his time and energy are visibly marked off into segments. If we get so much, someone else gets less, and if someone else gets such and such a portion, our share is thereby reduced.

God is not limited

Of course, God is not subject to the limitations of time and space that we know. We cannot apply to this case—to the Lord's love of his people—our standards of measurement. The love, the providence, the presence of God for his people is, as God is, infinite. As a result, the love or providence of God which one person may feel in life will in no way diminish love and providence for any other.

No reason for envy

This is what Paul tries to get across in today's selection from the Second Epistle to the Corinthians. We, as members of Christ's

Body, the Church, have no reason to feel envious of others who appear to prosper, spiritually or materially, when we do not feel we are so fortunate. In our terms, this will be a difficult lesson. It would appear, at first glance, that we have every reason to envy those who seem to feel more of God's providence than we do, at this or that particular time. After all, we are never so mindful of anyone's needs as we are of our own, and we are never so observant of our own good fortune as we are of others'.

We need to realize, however, that our own well-being can only enhance that of others, and that others' well-being can only add to our own. A distinguished American Catholic philosopher, Mary Rose Barral, has said that such things as knowledge and education—like love—cannot be had at another's expense, and that sharing them increases, rather than divides, these goods. The same, surely, is true of God's love and providence.

And for an earlier philosopher, we might turn to Confucius, who appeared to appreciate the same insight in saying, "He who wishes to secure the good of others has already secured his own."

Fourteenth Sunday of the Year

Both the first and last readings of today's liturgy show us the office and circumstances of the prophet. The first reading, from the Old Testament book of the prophet Ezekiel (Ez 2:2-5) shows the resistance of the people to God's Word sent through his messenger. The Gospel (Mk 6:1-6) shows Jesus as the prophet without honor in his country. The second reading (2 Cor 12:7-10) should serve to remind Christians that difficulty will be part of witness to the Lord Jesus.

Honor except at home

The image presented in today's Gospel should strike home in our society: the prophet who is not without honor—who is honored and revered and valued in so many places—*except* in his own "country" or "home town," or native region.

The situation which Jesus had to contend with is one familiar to many humans: familiarity itself seems to breed, if not contempt, at least an unwillingness to take seriously someone who is "one of the neighbors' children" or "part of the furniture," and whose measure is thus presumed, rather than calculated seriously.

"Glutted market"

The situation of the prophet seeking a position of credibility is aggravated even further in our own society today. Those regions which produce the greatest numbers of educated and qualified young people—teachers, writers, religious-educators, clergy, social service workers—sometimes have least need of them, because of a "glutted market" in these areas.

Most teachers today cannot exercise their chosen professions where they grew up and studied; many of them, today, even leave the country in search of employment. Many of today's clergy are people not needed where they came from, but needed in strange places; the same is often true of religious-educators and social service workers. Lawyers are beginning to find that they will have to relocate in order to deal with a growing availability of legal talent. Writers and others who would exercise intellectual leadership or creativity often find the same things: a lack of need for their services at home, and the necessity of moving to a strange place, serving and living among strange people.

Leaving home

The service professions are not unique in this. It is true of a variety of businesses and occupations, where the local economies of this place and that place cannot support their output of talent. This was the subject of an NBC-TV program several years ago, "Leaving Home Blues," which showed a number of southern high school graduates, white and black alike, who had to move north because there were no jobs anywhere near their town. The same phenomenon affects businessmen and executives, as Vance Packard pointed out in his recent book *A Nation of Strangers*. Packard, one of the better-known social analysts of our time, has pointed out the psychological and emotional damage done to people who are moved all over the map by the demands of their occupations, and he even shows how this can hurt the communities in which they relocate, politically and financially.

No immediate answer

There is no immediate answer for the prophet without honor in his or her own country, even in these times when that age-old human situation appears to be getting no better and, in fact, much worse.

What we can do, though, is be sensitive to those who would serve mankind and who, despite the best motivation and cooperation from strangers, will always need some support and respect from "their own." We can be receptive to those who may come to us seeking such endorsement and encouragement, whether from our own community or elsewhere.

We can, moreover, take to heart one of the verses of the popular folk-hymn "Whatsoever You Do": "In a strange country you made me at home; seeking employment, you found me a job."

We must respond to needs

One of the demands of all times, but especially of our own, is that we attend to the needs and wants and hurts of those who are displaced, relocated against their will, missing people, places and things that speak to them of who they are—or those who are in danger of facing such situations. We may not always be capable of preventing or changing such unhappy situations, but we can at least ease the pain they bring with them when they come, as members of a Christian community of love, concern and healing in the name of Jesus, who himself understood what it was to be a prophet without honor in his own country and among his own people.

Fifteenth Sunday of the Year

Today's readings, in the middle of a season of the year which should celebrate hope, seem to take account of man's tendency to feel oppressed or discouraged by the apparent sameness of everyday life and its problems. There is particular attention too, to a theme we have seen before: the rejected messenger of God, as seen with the Old Testament prophet (Am 7:12-15) and in the Gospel selection (Mk 6:7-13). As the Epistle points out, there is hope for God's messenger, in the Person of Jesus (Ep 1:3-14).

More difficulties

The Biblical themes of today's liturgical readings illustrate once more for us the difficulties that may be expected in following the Lord and his Way. This will tend, at times, to discourage even those who enthusiastically embrace Jesus and his Gospel, since it seems to thwart the happiness we expect to find by so doing.

The desire for happiness

It is a known fact of life that all people want to be happy. We want the best of life for our families, our friends and certainly for ourselves. And so, husbands and wives want love and conjugal harmony. Parents desire love, respect and obedience from their children. Children want guidance, understanding and patience from their parents. The engaged want acceptance, mutual respect and the security of knowing that their love is lasting.

Teachers want cooperation, respect and dedicated work from their students. Students want justice, encouragement and good guidance from their teachers. And, of course, all of us want, no matter what our vocation may be, peace of mind, a clean conscience and especially the feeling that we are loved.

But, from time to time, we meet obstacles that disturb us, obstacles that hold us back from being happy. We feel the weight of our human nature, we feel the sharp criticism of others. Without a doubt, we sin, and our sins hurt others. Also, we feel the pain of sins committed against us. Life, at last, can be a definite struggle at times against our own weaknesses and against the hypocrisy and self-love of certain people we meet.

Christians must hope

But, if we are true Christians, we have hope! By reading the Gospel, we can see that Jesus Christ was not always accepted. In fact, we learn in the Gospel according to Luke (4:24) that the people of Nazareth, the city where Jesus was raised, did not accept him. His own townsmen rejected him, and he, with self-respect and without embarrassment, said: "A prophet is without honor in his own land."

Again, we need hope! Jesus Christ was not only true God but also true man, and he suffered much from being misunderstood and criticized. But he never renounced his sacred mission. He carried through to fulfillment the will of his Father in spite of obstacles. We should use him as an example of patience, perseverance and hope.

We should come to know the person of Jesus more intimately. We must convince ourselves that in Jesus Christ, God comes to be our friend and faithful brother. This is the vocation of all who call themselves Christians.

Jesus was rejected

When things, events, persons or even ourselves cause us difficulty, we must remember Jesus Christ and how he was rejected by his own townsmen, his own kind and how he was crucified by the very people whom he came to help and redeem.

If we possess the strength and love of Jesus—obtained through the sacraments of the Church, the reading of the Scriptures, fervent prayer and a Christian way of life—we are better able to withstand the difficulties that bother us.

If we hold ever-present the example Jesus gave us, we can say with confidence the same words of St. Paul, a man who definitely lived in the presence of Jesus and who imitated him faithfully: "And that is why I am quite happy with my weaknesses, and with insults, hardships, persecutions, and the agonies I go through for Christ's sake. For it is when I am weak that I am strong." (2 Cor 12:10)

The above remarks are based on an article "Mantenga la Esperanza" by Rev. John A. Quill of St. Mary's Parish, Jersey City, N.J., published in the Spanish edition of *The Advocate* (Archdiocese of Newark, N.J.), and translated by Ann Holt. © 1974 by *The Advocate*; reprinted with permission.

Sixteenth Sunday of the Year

The Old Testament reading, from the book of the prophet Jere-miah (Jr 23:1-6) insists that shepherds lead their flocks on only the right path, as in the example of the Lord provided in the Responsorial Psalm (Ps 23:1-3, 3-4, 5, 6). The same image comes through in the Gospel's presentation of Jesus as teacher (Mk 6: 30-34). It is in this very Jesus, Paul tells the Ephesians in the epistle (2:13-18), that men will find peace.

Images of tranquility

The Biblical sources we concentrate on in today's celebration of the Word of God, in our liturgy, present comforting images: we are led to think of kindly shepherds, security, peace and rest. We are encouraged to envision notions of tranquility, order, goodness, and other such things which we all wish would be more in evidence in our world and our lives.

Where does real peace come from? Only from the Lord Jesus, who reconciles us to God the Father and to one another, Paul tells us and our fellow Christians in that early community at Ephesus.

Real peace

True peace will come, though, to only those who really seek it. And the peace that is to be found is the peace which results from a genuine knowledge of our sharing in the mission and the resurrection of the Lord Jesus.

To seek this knowledge, and the peace that will result from it, will not be easy. This will especially be so in light of the fact that there are many possible directions one might follow in the quest of peace, and knowledge and understanding, in the Lord Jesus.

But the path which actually should be followed is no false way; rather, it is the Way of Christ himself. We see, today, in the Biblical passages of the liturgy, the notion of the Lord as a shepherd, who leads his flock on only the right path, toward those things that will help them, and away from all harm.

How are we to know that path? We have often been told that we know that path when we hold to the teachings of the Church. But even then, there is difficulty in learning just what it is that the Church teaches, or just who is able to speak for or in the name of the Church. It is, as the King of Siam said in the play, "a puzzlement!"

Criteria for Church teaching

There are numerous criteria that are important. One of them is stressed in today's Biblical images: the good shepherd keeps the sheep together, and does not scatter them apart, we learn from the prophet Jeremiah. Moreover, Paul tells us through the Epistle to the Ephesians, Christ is the one who tears down barriers.

In the early Church, Paul and the others who taught in Jesus' name, with Peter at their head, strove always to present the true message of the Lord in such a way as to unite men in Christ, and not to divide them. Sometimes, of course, it was necessary for the Apostles—the first bishops in the Church—to exclude some persons from the life of the community if they persisted in serious violations of the Gospel (idolatry, adultery, and the like). But with such an obvious exception—when some directly worked against Jesus' teachings—the tendency was to see if people could be brought together, and not scattered apart, in the name of Christ.

The first heretics in the history of the Church were excluded from the total community because, ironically enough, they attempted to exclude others. Some of the early heretics were Gnostics, who claimed that they possessed a special sort of knowledge not available to all. Some other early heretics were Judaizers, who held that even Gentiles (non-Jews) wishing to accept Jesus and his Gospel would first have to embrace the Mosaic Law of Judaism. Both of these groups in the early history of Christianity tried to construct a religion which was too exclusive. By so doing, they brought about their own separation from the Body of Christ, and the Greek term for such a separation gives rise to our English word "heresy."

What Catholic means

In the early history of the Church we see mention of the term —again from the Greek—"Catholic," meaning universal. One who would be considered Catholic, as distinct from the heretics, would be one who believed as did the Church universal, and who held as did the Church in all times and all places. The heretic, or one who would not conform to the designation "Catholic," would be one quick to embrace a peculiar doctrine or interpretation, holding sway in only one period of time or one region, mistaking that for what the whole Church should always and everywhere be or teach.

There are other criteria for finding the real path of the good shepherd, which can be explored in turn. But one which comes to us clearly, in today's Scriptural lessons, is that the good shepherd brings about peace insofar as he gathers the sheep together, and does not divide or scatter them.

Seventeenth Sunday of the Year

The first reading (2 K 4:42-44) is the first in a series of Biblical selections which show the tendency of Scriptural images to develop "types" or notions which are intensified or further explicated in later stages; so it is with the Gospel passage (Jn 6:1-15), where the bread Jesus gives to the crowds fulfills the "hint" contained in the Old Testament historical literature. The Epistle selection, taken once more from Paul's letter to the Ephesians, underscores the fact that only in Jesus is there real peace.

Being taken care of

One of the first things people think of, naturally enough, is being taken care of physically, and particularly in terms of being fed. It was not all that long ago that one American President, referring to the military campaign in Indochina, promised that the nation could afford "both guns and butter" . . . and one of his predecessors in office, some years prior, was known for the slogan "a chicken in every pot."

Small wonder, then, that when man sets about to seeing his religious experiences and insights recorded in tradition, first orally and in the Scriptures, there should be emphasis on being fed. We see this, in our first reading today, in the historical literature of the Old Testament, as reflected in the second book of Kings. And the image of feeding is fulfilled, in the Gospel narrative we have in today's liturgy, according to John, with Jesus feeding the multitudes.

Public relations?

One of the lessons implied in the Gospel story is that Jesus' audience was in danger of misunderstanding the meaning of what happened. They were apt to view him as some one who would provide for them materially, and in such a way as to make them have him as a political or temporal ruler. In this way, perhaps, to use our own experience as an analogy, we might say that some of those who were at Tiberias' shore that day tended to view the occurrence there as something of a campaign rally or public-relations exercise on Jesus' part. And like many people in many a crowd, there were those who were quick to follow Jesus and proclaim his name so long as they thought that by so doing they would ensure that their own material needs were taken care of. It is from exactly that type of thing that Jesus is depicted as fleeing, for that was not the meaning of either his preaching or his kingdom.

The meaning is brought out in the Epistle selection for today, as expressed by Paul the Apostle to the Church of the Ephesians in the first century of Christian history: faith and baptism in the Lord . . . "who is over all, and works through all, and is in all."

This does not mean that Christianity never attends to human needs on a physical level or in a practical way. If anything, the social teachings of the Church in the moral order would indicate quite the opposite. The Body of Christ, the Church, like Christ himself, will realize that man has both physical and spiritual needs, and will therefore try to meet both, whenever possible.

But the chief goal of Jesus is to meet those needs which are deepest in the human situation, and of the more enduring sort, namely the need of human beings to be at one with one another and with their heavenly Father, in "one body and one Spirit . . ." as Paul puts it.

Spiritual nourishment

And therefore the nourishment which we will need will be not only physical but spiritual. Moreover, the nourishment that will be required for the life of the Body of Christ, the Church, will be sacramental, since the Church itself, as sign of the presence of the Lord in the world, is a sort of sacrament.* The bread the Church will thrive on will be not merely the sort of bread Elisha gave to his people, or even the kind Jesus fed the crowds with on the shore of Tiberias, but—as we know—this bread will be the bread which is the sacramental Body of Christ in the Eucharist.

By partaking of the Eucharist we both add to and celebrate our union with God the Father, through Jesus his Son, in the Holy Spirit. More than that is evident, too, for we also add to and celebrate our unity with one another in Christ, as members of his Body the Church. This is the food, this Eucharistic bread, which gives life to each of us individually, and to all of us as members of the community of the Lord which is the Church. And nourished by this bread, we will be called upon, as Paul reminds the Ephesians and through them all Christians, to "... live a life worthy of (membership in the Eucharistic community), with perfect humility, meekness and patience, bearing with one another lovingly."

---

*Cf. E. Schillebeeckx, *Christ the Sacrament of the Encounter with God* (New York: Sheed & Ward, Inc., 1963), tr. Cornelius Ernst, Chs. 1, 2.

Eighteenth Sunday of the Year

The Old Testament reading which begins the series for today's liturgy narrates the dissatisfaction of the pilgrim Hebrews (Ex 16:2-4, 12-15) and God's providence for them in the desert. (This occurrence is now believed to have been caused naturally, but to the People of God, it was "miraculous" as a sign of Yahweh's care for them.) In the Gospel (Jn 6:24-35), Jesus distinguished between the bread of heaven and that other bread which his followers might be apt to expect. Paul, in the second reading (Ep 4: 17, 20-24), once more calls upon Christians to live lives consistent with their religious identity.

Moving is never easy

Moving is never an easy experience for anyone. We move for a variety of reasons, usually to bring about some improvement in our lives: a larger home, or one better suited to our needs, or in a nicer location, or more convenient to work, school or other elements that are important in our lives. Usually, even though we are sad to leave a familiar place which we have come to call "home," we look with optimistic anticipation to the new place to which we are going. We visualize all the things which attracted us to the new location in the first place, and in our mind's eye, we even see the new home decorated as we would have it, with our favorite pieces of furniture or mementos in special places we have already selected mentally. On the other hand, we look, usually with some fondness, upon the "old place," seeing once again everything in a particular pattern.

But, as anyone who has moved would know, there is not a simple transition from the one to the other! Instead, there is a long, tiring, often even frustrating, period of packing, and cleaning, and searching, and rearranging, and loading, so that the place we have come to accept as home for so long a period of time is now somewhat a shambles. And on the other end, it is no better! The new home is at best barren and bleak, not yet "lived in," except perhaps by strangers. So many things that must be done to make it a home have yet to be accomplished. In the mean time, there are boxes and crates and things still on their way. And, as most people who have ordered any new furniture are aware, we seldom receive deliveries at the time or on the day promised.

A move begun must be completed

Circumstances like these are enough to make most people despair of moving, and possibly wish they had stayed put in the first place. But, as we know, once a move is begun, it must be completed. Besides, we make the move because we believe it is a good one for us. But, during the time of transition, how we so often wish we had never begun the move at all, and we would —so many times—be perfectly willing to turn back the clock and calendar, and settle for things as they had been before, much as we know that is really impossible.

The Israelites in the desert

This was how the Israelites felt, from what the book of Exodus narrates in today's first reading, when they were en route from bondage in Egypt to the Promised Land. Life under the Pharaoh had been hard, and by no means attractive. Yet it was more attractive, by comparison, than life in the desert, which is where the People of Israel were after they got out of Egypt. And, of course, there was no going back. Very understandably, faced with the rigors and deprivations of life in the desert,

"The whole Israelite community grumbled against Moses

and Aaron. The Israelites said to them, 'Would that we had died at the Lord's hand in the land of Egypt, as we sat by our fleshpots and ate our fill of bread! But you had to lead us into this desert to make the whole community die of famine!' "

As we read later in the same passage, the Lord provided nourishment for his People and took care of them. But, until such time as that intervention, and other signs of the providence of the God who guided his People to their Promised Land, one could understand their feelings of frustration and, perhaps most vexing of all, their inability to turn back.

We who have been called to make a transition in following Jesus, in his New Covenant, may often feel as though we would have been more comfortable in familiar complacency or ignorance: it would be so much easier if we didn't know all that we know now, enlightened as we have been by the Holy Spirit. But if we feel this way, it is because, like the Israelites in the desert, and all others "on the move," we have yet to see everything come into place. We must then see it in our mind's eye, keeping in our consciousness the promises of the Lord that he will take care of his People.

Nineteenth Sunday of the Year

The first reading, from the Old Testament books of Kings (1 K 19:4-8), provides a lesson in perseverance under the guidance of the Lord. In the second selection, from the Epistle to the Ephesians, we see basically the same theme, precised in this case with specific types of attitudes and actions to cultivate and avoid (Ep 4:30-5:2). The Gospel passage (Jn 6:41-51) assures us that no one can come to the Father except through his Son, Jesus.

"Slack season"

This series of liturgical readings comes to us in the middle, roughly, of the "Sundays of the Year" in the Church's calendar, and in just about the middle—give or take a little—of the summertime. We are in the middle of vacations from school, with the old term long finished and the new one nearly about to begin. This is for many businesses a "slack season," and many institutions and services slow down into a "summer schedule." We are, probably, no longer feeling the excitement of a June which—according to Oscar Hammerstein's lyric—"comes bustin' out all over," or the briskness of fall. We are a long way from the major holidays, beginning with Labor Day, that punctuate with emphasis the latter months of a year.

Dull sameness

In short, we find ourselves at a time of year when "not much seems to be happening" in or around our lives and homes, at

least generally speaking. Sometimes, even the weather can bring
a kind of dull sameness to the season we are in presently. It is
a time of year when we can become bored, discouraged, or
"down in the dumps." Is it any wonder that so many people
choose this time of year for a vacation, to "get away from it all"
and come back to everyday life refreshed?

Perhaps we need some spiritual and intellectual refreshment
at this time, too, and for that reason we are fortunate in the
Church's choice of Biblical readings for the liturgy today. Like
Elijah, of whom we read in the first Book of Kings in the Old
Testament, we need to be prodded on by the messenger of the
Lord. And, as Paul will remind us through the Ephesians, we
must do nothing to "sadden the Holy Spirit" who is the source
of our lives and energies as members of the Body of Christ.

This is why we are reminded to cultivate those outlooks, and
those outward actions, which stem from those lives and energies.
Even when tired or discouraged, we are reminded, we must be
"kind to one another, compassionate and mutually forgiving,"
resisting all of the temptations—even very strong ones at times—
to lapse into "bitterness, . . . passion and anger, harsh words,
slander and malice of every kind." Of course, it is easy, particularly in a time of discouragement or dullness, to lapse into just
such feelings. Perhaps things are not going as we feel they should
in our lives. It becomes incredibly easy to blame others, or to
feel envious of them. We can so easily make other people the
targets for our feelings of frustration, which we are unable to
meet "head on" or cope with directly, often because we cannot
really recognize such feelings for just what they are.

It is easy, too, to become short-tempered, irritable, "hard
to live with" in general. Once more, we will need to persevere,
in faith and hope, and try to see things as they really are, in
some kind of perspective. The Lord, we know, will help us to do
this if we cooperate with the help he provides in the Holy Spirit.

A chance for a "break"

Of course, the help which comes from God the Father can

come to us only through Jesus, as we are reminded in today's selection from the Gospel according to John. And we encounter Jesus in the presence he affords us in many ways—including the Word of God in the liturgy and in the Bible generally—but most importantly in the Eucharist. There is an old saying that the summertime may mean vacation from many things, but never from one's religious life and obligations. This approach is negative. It makes more sense, perhaps, to view the situation *positively*: Because summer allows us a vacation or "break" from some other elements in life, there is a good opportunity to increase and deepen our appreciation of Christ's saving presence in Word and Eucharist. And, like Elijah, if we need nourishment to continue on the journey of life, let us take it. And the nourishment we take can be the "bread of life . . . the bread that comes down from heaven, for a man to eat and never die. . . . If anyone eats this bread he shall live forever. . . ."

Twentieth Sunday of the Year

The first reading (Pr 9:1-6) utilizes a common device in Old Testament sapiential literature, personification (in this case of Wisdom). Our Epistle selection, once more from Ephesians, continues to remind Christians to carefully discharge the obligations of membership in Christ's Body (Ep 5:15-20). In the Gospel, we again turn to the Johannine account (Jn 6:51-58), and a continuation of the panem vitae *discourse.*

Wisdom, age and youth

The image of wisdom is usually an image of old age. In thinking of wisdom, we often tend to envision an old man with tired eyes, smoking his pipe and contemplating the state of the world and the meaning of life, concerned for it all, yet convinced that "there is nothing new under the sun."

Not long ago, a young girl named Joyce Maynard published an article in *The New York Times Magazine* under the title, "An 18-Year-Old Looks Back on Life." And, in fact, the article contained much wisdom. The point of the article seemed to be that one need not be advanced in years to have experienced a great deal in life, and to be able to reflect upon it all, with some ability to understand the meanings behind the events.

One element in Joyce Maynard's thinking is that those who were born, as she was, after World War II or the Korean War, have seen so much at so early an age in life—largely by virtue of television—that they do indeed have much to remember and reflect on by the time they are eighteen or so. This does not necessarily mean, of course, that the experiences will be reflected on with balance and insight. And a case can surely be made for the other possible implication: those who see much in a short period of time may lack the perspective required for proper evaluation.

But be that as it may, wisdom is not simply a matter of "length of days" in life. One can be ancient, yet ignorant. One can be young, yet possess a certain wisdom that is surprising.

Biblical view of wisdom

What does the Bible tell of wisdom? In today's first reading, from the Book of Proverbs in the Old Testament, we see Wisdom personified, welcoming all who would seek understanding, and beckoning to all who would avoid foolishness. In a word, we could say, wisdom resides in seeing things in proper alignment, and giving stress to the right priorities.

The same concept is brought out, perhaps more explicitly, in our second reading, from Paul's letter to the Church at Ephesus: "Do not act like fools, but like thoughtful men. Make the most of the present opportunity. . . ." The perspective the early Christians—and ourselves—will be encouraged to develop is one which sees lasting priorities as important, and does not lapse into momentary goals.

Long-range thinking

Another way of putting this, in contemporary terms, is that the wise person does a good deal of "long-range" thinking. "What is *really* important? What is of *lasting* value? What difference will this make five years from today? *Ten* years from today? At the end of my life? Even after my life has ended?" Questions like these must be asked and answered in the alignment of goals and priorities. And the criteria in questioning are indicative of the perspective, the "long view" that comes with wisdom.

It is for such reasons that we do tend to associate wisdom

with age, for the young often are inexperienced in life and with taking the measure of the world. Youth, often, tends to carry with it a sense of immediacy: today's history exam, this week's game, the big party on Saturday. But the old are capable of being just as short-sighted, and the young are capable of astounding their elders with wisdom. The important thing is the development of a vision which goes beyond the immediate, and is therefore able to see things over-all, each in terms of its ultimate meaning and value.

It is this kind of wisdom we are encouraged to seek: "Forsake foolishness that you may live; advance in the way of understanding."

Twenty-first Sunday of the Year

The first reading (Jos 24:1-2, 15-17, 18) calls upon the People of God to recognize and serve their One God and no other. They have no alternative, nor do the followers of Jesus in the Covenant that comes, as seen in the Gospel (Jn 6: 60-69). The second reading is a familiar one, illustrating the value of Christian marriage as a sign of the love between Christ and his Body on earth, the Church (Ep 5:21-32).

Submission hardly popular today

To most of us, submission seems hardly a virtue. Even our popular literature, these days, tells us to "be our own best friend" and to strike out on our own, for ourselves. For at least this reason, today's reading from St. Paul's letter to the Ephesians may be unattractive.

The dignity of woman

But there is even more at stake, of course, in this famous New Testament passage. The imagery commonly inferred is of a passive wife submitting in her married life to a dominant husband, to the point where this might seem to compromise or endanger the dignity of woman—always important, but especially stressed as important today.

What many people fail to realize, however, is that this passage is actually safeguarding the dignity of woman in the historical context of its time. It is a balanced statement, calling upon the husband to give over his very life for the protection of his wife and family. This may not sound revolutionary in our time. But in those days it was important for the Judaeo-Christian tradition to rebuke the attitudes of the pagan world which so often neglected the dignity of woman and her need to be regarded as a person in marriage.

A special sign

The way in which a man gives himself to his wife—and the way in which a woman gives herself to her husband—will be significant in terms of the mutual respect and responsibility involved. This is what makes marriage, as we know it, different from any other type of arrangement, relationship or "alternative life-style." This is what makes marriage in the Lord a saving sign, or sacrament, witnessed and celebrated in the Christian community of the Church.

Learning the hard way

Many people, particularly young people, have tended of late to doubt the value of marriage. Often they have asked, quite sincerely, "Why not just live together? Why a formal ritual? Who needs a piece of paper?" In one sense, they would be right in criticizing ritual which is empty, or pieces of paper which are merely legalistic. But that is not the same thing as criticizing the Christian institution of marriage which relies on human love and divine grace. And many of these young people, or some of their friends or acquaintances, of late, have been learning that certain alternative relationships are unfulfilling, unsatisfactory, and even destructive within a fragile human life and spirit, male or female. They are possibly learning, the hard way, the value of marriage as we know it in the community of faith and sacramental life which is the Church.

Different but similar

Some of the young people celebrating their commitment in

marriage, according to the rites of the Church, may do this in a way which is puzzling to many of us today. They have, often, guitars rather than organ music. And, frequently, they choose one of the alternative Scripture readings the Church provides, rather than the traditional Epistle heard today. But when such people commit themselves to each other in Christ, they are committing themselves to be signs of love in and for the Christian community, in a fashion which is externally different in some ways, but internally similar, in comparison with their elders. And as members of the same community of faith and celebration, we wish them well in the name of the Lord.

Twenty-second Sunday of the Year

The first reading (Dt 4:1-2, 6-8) *demonstrates the importance the Old Covenant would attach to the observance of the Law of the Lord. The second reading* (Jm 1:17-18, 21-22, 27) *shows that not only the authority of law, but "Every worthwhile gift ... comes from (the Lord)...." In the Gospel* (Mk 7:1-8, 14-15, 21-23), *excessive observance of the Mosaic Law is exemplified in the Pharisees and deplored by Jesus.*

Law essential in society

Law is essential to any society, to structure it and keep it operating efficiently. There is a danger in lawlessness, or too little legal protection. There is also a danger in too much legal structure, or "big government" which becomes overwhelming. As President Ford said to the Congress, just after his inauguration in 1974, the government big enough to give you everything you want is big enough to take away everything you have. All Americans, regardless of their political persuasion or party, are sensitive to the problems brought about by too little—or too much—law. So it is with men in every nation. For individuals of any political stripe, it is a difficult dilemma to work with, in any country or system: how much law will be oppressive, and stop the society from functioning as it should, and how little law will result in anarchy and chaos?

A dilemma

The same dilemma was presented to the Israelites in the Old

Covenant. And in our first reading, from the book of Deuteronomy, we see testimony to their appreciation of the Law which came to them by the providence of God, through Moses, to give order and life to Israel as both a nation and a religious society.

By the time of Jesus' earthly ministry, though, we see that a number of people take the Law too literally, or extend it too strictly. The group that did this most conspicuously are familiar to us as Pharisees. These were teachers and students of the Law who sincerely loved the Law so much that they would do all they could to comply with every one of its prescriptions and prohibitions. Unfortunately, the tendency they cultivated was in the direction of obeying every detail of human tradition about the observance of the Law, in such a way as to lose sight of their genuine obligations to God. To use a popular expression, they failed to see the forest for the trees.

"Setting them straight"

In the Gospel narrative we read today, Jesus is depicted as "setting them straight." His words, according to Mark, draw attention where it properly belongs: not to the trivial observances of human ritual or prescription, but to the basic demands of the moral law of God.

In the Church today, as in society generally, there is still a danger of being too legalistic, or on the other hand of being anarchistic. There is, too, the danger of applying the law to others but not ourselves. As we learned in the "Watergate" scandals, many "law and order" men considered themselves excepted from legal obligations and prohibitions.

"Rule-of-thumb"

We need hardly go through all the examples and ramifications of these questions here and now, but let us concentrate on this criterion or "rule-of-thumb": What does God teach, clearly, about my obligations? What am I doing, as best I can, honestly and sincerely, to live up to my moral obligations? If we can answer frankly, without attempting to cover up for ourselves, and without being scrupulous or too hard on ourselves, we shall have come a long way.

One way of helping to deal with such questions might be this: Are we performing actions because they are seen by others, and are we concerned with what people will think or say about us? This appears to be an important element in the Gospel passage for today. The elements of the Law which the Pharisees were quick to observe were often external rituals, able to be observed outwardly, like those described in the Gospel account. The elements of moral obligation Jesus spoke to in the same account are mostly matters of internal moral disposition, which can be hidden from public view.

It was possible for the Pharisees, and others, to perform ritual actions which might gain them the admiration or praise of the community, all the while hiding grievously immoral attitudes, and actions resulting from these attitudes, in their private lives. To paraphrase today's Epistle from James, acting in humble charity and conscientious fairness will "make for pure worship without stain before our God and Father."

Twenty-third Sunday of the Year

The first reading, from the Old Testament book of Isaiah (Is 35:4-7) encourages those who wait for divine vindication; this is a frequent Old Testament prophetic theme. In the second reading, from the epistle attributed to James in the New Testament (Jm 22: 1-5), vindication takes on the dimension of reward for the poor in the world. The Gospel seems to expand on the same theme, but with a particular stress on attention to the physical needs of the sick (Mk 7:31-37).

Success and failure

The message of today's Biblical texts in the liturgy, like so many others, is clear: those who appear to fail in this world will in reality succeed in the eyes of the Lord, who will bring vindication to them, and those who appear to succeed in the world will in fact fail, if they do not follow the ways of the Lord.

This message brought great encouragement for the People of God in the Old Testament, since they were so often on the lowest rung of the ladder, socio-economically. Their lives were hard, and they did not enjoy the sort of prosperity which could be seen in so many of the societies around them.

This theme expands, of course, in the New Covenant of Jesus, who concerns himself so much and so often with the needs of those who are sick and often neglected. Though they appear to find only misfortune in this life, the Lord wants to assure them that they are dear to him and deserve his attention.

Society stresses "winning"

If we are Christ in the world, in his body the Church, then we, too, are obliged to demonstrate concern for the sick and the neglected. And, as was the case with the Israelites of old, we will find that the society around us hardly encourages us in this direction. Our society, after all, places such great emphasis on "winning," on "being on top," on "coming out ahead" or "being number one," that there seems little room or concern left over for the sick, the poor, the elderly, or those who might otherwise be neglected or disadvantaged.

We live, we are so often reminded, in a culture dominated by images of youth and "the beautiful people." We spend millions upon millions of dollars a year to keep looking young, even without improving our physical health, by means of creams, corsets, dyes and devices of every sort. We each find ourselves compared to the most glamorous specimens around us, held up to the ideal norms. We are, in a word, perhaps intimidated by constant emphasis on images of beauty and youth.

There is, of course, nothing at all wrong with being young, as we all are at one time, or with possessing the gift of physical beauty. But, the question must be raised, what of those among us who, through no fault at all of their own, are neither young nor beautiful? What of those who are not in good health? Are these to be cast aside, rejected as misfits in a society of beauty and youth and fitness? All too often, in our culture, the answer seems to be "yes."

The follower of the Lord and his Way, however, will realize that neither beauty nor youth are required for admission to the kingdom. Indeed, those who do not enjoy riches, youth, beauty, health or the other "good things" we so often hear and see stressed in life, are the very ones whom the Lord cares about in a special way. By no means does the Lord or his followers seek to *cultivate* poor health, or poverty, or deprivation. But he realizes that an infirm or poor person, so often rejected by our culture, is a very important person indeed.

Each person has dignity

Each person has a special dignity in the Lord which comes from within, not from without, owing to his being a creature of God. Each member of the body of Christ enjoys a special importance by virtue of his or her membership in the Church. And each member of that body has a responsibility to those who are in need of care, attention, solicitude.

This is a good occasion, in the light of today's Scriptural lessons, to examine our consciences, individually and as a community, concerning our attitudes and actions—or in some cases our *lack* of actions—regarding the poor, the sick, the others whom our society would be quick to shun. We need to ask ourselves, "Am I responding to this person, in this situation, as the Lord would?" If the answer is "no," then we may well be in step with a prevalent attitude in contemporary society, but that will hardly be to our credit. If our answer is that we *are* striving to put Christian attitudes into practice, then we will come to know a final divine vindication, of the sort described in today's Biblical texts.

As James asks us: "Did not God choose those who are poor in the eyes of the world to be rich in faith and heirs of the kingdom he promised to those who love him?"

Twenty-fourth Sunday of the Year

The first reading, from the book of the Old Testament prophet Isaiah (Is 50:4-9), is a declaration of God's providence for and protection of his messengers in the face of the difficulties they will necessarily encounter. But to profess the faith, alone, without practicing it concretely, will not suffice, as our second reading (Jm 2:14-18) makes abundantly clear. To be a follower of the Lord, in proclaiming and practicing his Word, will bring suffering in the eyes of men, according to Mark's account of the Gospel (Mk 8:27-35).

Principles hard to practice

To be a follower of Jesus involves two basic modes of operation: practicing the principles of the Gospel, and communicating them to others, that they too might embrace and practice the same principles. As James stresses in our second reading today, it will not be enough simply to proclaim God's word without acting upon it concretely. We must put the principles into practice, each one of us according to his or her actual circumstances and opportunities in life. In fact, by this very action we will be proclaiming, or exhibiting, the Word of God. But acting upon, and uttering, the Word of God will cause us to pay prices in this world, and that notion runs through the Biblical lessons for the liturgy today.

The unpopular Gospel

The book of the prophet Isaiah, from the Old Testament,

expresses these truths by saying that the messenger of the Lord will give his back to those who beat him, his cheeks to those who pluck his beard, and his face to even those who would spit in it. Or as one modern-day priest put it not long ago, someone truly committed to practicing and preaching the Gospel should "put a brass plate inside the seat of his pants, and let them keep on kicking!" In any terms, or by anyone's lights, the preaching of the Gospel, and the practicing of its principles, will be unpopular simply because the Gospel calls upon us to be less selfish, less arrogant, less immature in our persons and in our ways of living.

Jesus pointed these things out in his earthly ministry, as narrated by today's selection from the Gospel according to Mark: "He . . . began to teach them that the Son of Man had to suffer much, be rejected by the elders, the chief priests, and the scribes, be put to death. . . . He said this quite openly." Of course, we can appreciate the fact that Jesus' death actually culminates in his resurrection (as the Gospel account also tells us). We realize, too, that the parties and persons who opposed Jesus' teachings were in error. But this does not alter the fact that the religious and social leaders of that period and place were capable of intimidating and ostracizing the followers of Jesus, and of making life very difficult for them. And, in many cases, this difficult life ended in death at the hands of those who had opposed the Gospel of Jesus all along.

The only real defense

There can be no real defense against that sort of ostracism, punishment or persecution, short of a deep and genuine faith in and commitment to the Lord, of the sort described by the prophet in our initial reading for this liturgy:

"The Lord God is my help, therefore I am not disgraced;
I have set my face like flint, knowing that I shall not be
    put to shame. . . .
See, the Lord God is my help; who'll prove me wrong?. . . ."

But make no mistake! These words are not meant to imply that the Lord will bring to his followers and messengers a vindication in their own time in the world. Nor does it mean that their adversaries will be humiliated for all to see in the here-and-now. The vindication that the bearer of the Gospel will know will come not from without in terms of human respect in the world, but from within in terms of that peace which comes from the Lord alone.

And those who follow the Way of the Lord, and share it with others, will find that, as their faith commitments mature, some priorities which once seemed paramount will tend to fade into relative insignificance, and new ones will supplant them. As Jesus tells his disciples in the Gospel: "Whoever would save his life will lose it, but whoever loses his life for my sake and the gospel's will save it."

Twenty-fifth Sunday of the Year

The lesson communicated by the first reading (Ws 2:12, 17-20) *should be no surprise, in light of the whole of revealed Salvation-History: wisdom and justice will be repugnant to the wicked of the world, who must campaign actively against the truth and goodness. But wisdom, characterized further in the second reading* (Jm 3:16-4:3), *is always innocent of guile, always peaceable. Contrary to the spirit of wisdom and goodness will be "status-seeking," as Jesus points out in the Gospel narrative according to Mark* (Mk 9:30-37).

Virtue is punishable

It does not take long, it does not require extensive studies in the ways of the world, to realize that being truthful, innocent, kind, courageous and consistent can be seriously punishable offenses. The just one, as described today by the Old Testament book of Wisdom, is obnoxious to the wicked, who feel they must "condemn him to a shameful death." Jesus, the Just One who comes in the New Testament, is acutely aware of this, as we see from today's Gospel according to Mark: "He was teaching his disciples in this vein: 'The Son of Man is going to be delivered into the hands of men who will put him to death. . . .' "

We know, of course, from the further explication of Jesus' teaching, that the same Son of Man, the same Christ, would rise three days after being put to death, bringing to fruition the words of the wisdom literature of old: ". . . if the just one be the son of God, he will defend him and deliver him from the hand of his foes." But in our own Christian lives, on an every-day basis, the resurrection of Jesus and our eventual sharing in it will be only a sort of *ultimate* consolation, at times, difficult to translate into *immediate* terms. We know, if we are members of Christ, that we can share in his final victory over sin and death, and all the limitations of "the human condition." But those very limitations, day after day, have a way of nagging at us and dragging us down as we try to live life in Christ Jesus.

Natural resistance to Wisdom

We will encounter, on an almost daily basis, such enemies as envy, pride, jealous sabotage, high-handedness, arrogance, avarice—and, most frustrating of all, we will encounter these in the Church itself, in even our closest friends and relatives, in even our very selves. If this is the case, and all too often it is, it is because no one, including ourselves, is anxious to put on such virtues as humility, meekness, selflessness and sacrifice which are required to live a really Christian life. So we, and those around us, will have a sort of natural resistance to Wisdom and the Just One, however much we call upon the name of the Lord, and however quick we might be to proclaim our member-ship in his Church.

James addressed himself to this kind of living in his letter to fellow Christians at the beginning of Church history: "Where do the conflicts and disputes among you originate? Is it not your inner cravings that make war within your members? . . . . You envy and you cannot acquire, so you quarrel and fight. You do not obtain because you do not ask. You ask and you do not receive because you ask wrongly, with a view to squan-dering what you receive on your pleasures."

All of us who are members of Christ's Church are subject to the pitfalls James describes. All of us who are members of Christ's Church are encouraged by the Scriptures today to think less of ourselves and our own personal "hang-ups" and more of the wisdom coming from the Lord. We must strive, James teaches us, to live lives which are not full of guile but innocent. Innocence does not mean ignorance. On the contrary, the innocent person can and often should know exactly what is going on around himself or herself. But the innocent person is not a party to evil actions, plans or motives.

We must also cultivate, habitually, in our lives those other virtues of which James' pastoral letter speaks. We must therefore be ". . . lenient, docile, rich in sympathy and the kindly deeds that are . . . impartial and sincere." Or as Jesus is reported as teaching his disciples in the Gospel according to Mark, we must have no concern for our "rank" or "status," or whatever honor may come our way in the world, even in the community of the Church. For when Jesus' followers began to argue as to who was most important, he told them plainly: "If anyone wishes to rank first, he must remain the last one of all and the servant of all."

Abiding inconveniences

Being a true follower of Christ will mean abiding many inconveniences and indignities, at least. More often, it will mean tolerating many a direct insult, as well as numerous unintentional slights. It will mean, in addition, suffering the most bitter kind of rebuke when we proclaim the Gospel and try to live by it; in so doing we will challenge the "Establishment" as it holds sway in the world. In all of these experiences, we must try to bring others to Christ as best we can, as kindly, yet firmly, as we can, as revilement and torture put us to the test, trying our gentleness and patience for the sake of Jesus.

Twenty-sixth Sunday of the Year

The Old Testament reading rightly stresses that a gift from the Lord, in this case that of prophecy, is meant to be distributed among as many as the Lord chooses (Nb 11:25-29). The same implication comes through in the Gospel sayings attributed to Jesus (Mk 9:38-43). In the second reading, from the letter of James (Jm 5:1-6), we are warned against the hoarding of material goods.

"The best things in life are free!"

Some of us who are older can remember the song which contained the lyric, "The moon belongs to everyone; the best things in life are free!" During the Great Depression of the 1930's, many people appeared to have been consoled by a thought such as this. In many instances since that time, the song has been on the lips or in the minds of many people. This is explicitly the case when monetary, material or financial hardship is immediately a threat, as it has been for too many of us, too often, recently. But the idea behind the lyric is implicitly present in any time and place, and it is a good idea to keep in mind. This is, in a way, the theme of the Biblical readings for today's liturgy.

Perishable treasures

There are, we all know, treasures which are perishable. These are the kinds of goods James describes in his letter, which we read today: "...your fine wardrobe has grown moth-eaten, your gold and silver have corroded.... See what you have stored up for yourselves against the last days...." We all realize that we depend to some extent on the goods of the world in order to live and to provide to those for whom we might have responsibility. But we should keep in mind always the futility of trying to make ourselves wealthy in a way which resists all hazards and protects us from all dangers. It has been tried, again and again, but it cannot really be done.

Those gifts which are not so perishable or precarious are those special gifts which come from the Lord. We see these gifts exemplified in our first and third readings today. In the first reading, from the Old Testament book of Numbers, the gift illustrated is that of prophecy. In the third reading, from the Gospel according to Mark, the gift shown is that of casting out devils or demons. In both instances, there is shown a gift from the Lord, to be used in the service of men to the glory of God.

Jealousy

Unfortunately, some people have tended to think—as shown in our Biblical readings—a gift from the Lord should be hoarded in the same way that some people hoard material goods or monetary riches. The Scripture points out that this is not the right attitude at all. If someone else has a talent they are able to use, with seriousness, sincerity and effectiveness, in the name of the Lord, no one should feel threatened by that. That, of course, is easy to say, but it is not always an easy principle to live by. There are those, as the Gospel intimates, who are quick to try to discredit signs of the Spirit that are exhibited by others "...not of our company." There are Catholics who try to dismiss signs of the Spirit's grace that are exhibited through Protestants, and there are Jews and Gentiles who may be suspicious of a divine gift shown by others not of their own group. Even within the Church itself, there have been priests and members of religious orders who have been suspicious—or more likely a bit jealous—when talents or gifts become evident in fellow members of the People of God who are not part of the same group *within* the Church. In the American Church, for instance, there was great friction in the 1950's, when religious Brothers, then Sisters, began the professional study and teaching, alongside priests, of theology. In the 1960's, clergy and religious demonstrated the same suspicion towards lay Catholics, in the same way, and also with regard to lay leaders in the liturgy (commentators, lectors and the like). In the 1970's, we have seen suspicion of the gifts of the Spirit exercised by married clergymen in the diaconate, or extraordinary ministers (of the Eucharist, or ministers of music, etc.) who are married or who are women. Of course, this sort of thing is hardly a one-way street. There have always been those lay "leaders" who are suspiciously and jealously protecting what they see as their own "turf" against "clerical interference," and they sometimes resort to extreme opinions or tactics.

The Spirit's gifts are free

We must always and everywhere praise the Lord for any gift of the Spirit, wherever and whenever it may be in evidence. We surely do not need to abandon the legitimate distinctions between our own Roman Catholic communion and other Christian bodies. Nor those between Christians and persons who love God but do not accept Jesus as Savior. We do not need, either, to forget those proper distinctions between the roles of various ministers, in formal holy orders or not, married or celibate, of either sex, within the people of God. But we should never become as jealous or protective concerning the gifts of the Spirit as some people do concerning money and material goods. The Spirit's gifts are limitless. And the best things in life—the gifts of the Spirit—are free.

Twenty-seventh Sunday of the Year

The first reading, from the Old Testament book of Genesis, gives an account in the tradition of the Israelites for the institution of marriage and the dignity of the male and female sexes (Gn 2:18-24). The second reading, from the Epistle to the Hebrews, points out how Jesus was subject to the human experience of even death, and fully immersed in the "human condition" (Heb 2:9-11). The Gospel, according to Mark (Mk 10:2-16), provides a narration of Jesus' teaching on marriage and divorce.

Jesus changed death's meaning—and life's

There are many lessons that can be drawn from the Biblical readings of the liturgy for today. One that comes to us through every one of the readings is the dignity of that human experience, or "human situation" which the Son of God, Jesus, entered "in the flesh." As the Epistle to the Hebrews tells us, Jesus tasted even death, amid a variety of other human experiences. Jesus, in so doing, made death mean no longer a sign of man's separation from God the Father, but now possibly a sign of a person's dying in Christ, rising in a new life in God's grace. Jesus, moreover, made clear the dignity of human life and of various forms of human activity and experience. One aspect of human life and activity which Jesus lends particular importance to is marriage, as seen in today's Biblical texts for liturgical reading.

The importance and dignity of marriage, of course, would not simply come "out of the blue" in the time of Jesus. We can observe from simply our Old Testament lesson of today that the Jews, for centuries before Christ, considered the union of man and woman in marriage to be important and sacred, as ordained by God. In Jesus' earthly ministry, as indicated in part by the Gospel according to Mark today, he stressed the sacredness of marriage in a sacramental way. The same stress was to be articulated by Jesus' Apostles, particularly Paul (for instance, in his Epistle to the Ephesians 5:21-32). This type of stress on the dignity of marriage directly aided people's understanding of the dignity of not only the male sex, but in particular the female sex.

Different views of woman

For some time during the history of both Judaism and Christianity, women had been considered as lesser human beings in comparison with men. Ignorance on various levels—psychological, physiological, intellectual—contributed to this understanding ... or actually misunderstanding ... of women. If truth be told, we have not completely erased such wrong notions from our society, even within the Christian community. But, with all its failings, that human institution of divine origin, the Church in her members, has been courageous, even revolutionary, at times, in defense of the dignity of women. Anyone who fails to understand this should consider the times in which Jesus, and his Apostles, preached and served among the people. Women tended to be considered as pieces of property, to be picked up and cast aside, or used and summarily dismissed, exploited and discarded, especially in the pagan culture that surrounded the Jews and the first Christians. The Judaic tradition tried to resist this way of thinking and acting, and so did Christianity in even its infancy. Jesus, in today's Gospel narration, is seen as resisting this erroneous viewpoint with special vigor, in defending the sacredness of the marriage bond, with a view to the dignity of male and female spouses alike. But in the circumstances of his times, Jesus' words would have special importance for women, who were in particular danger of being victims in divorce, as in numerous other situations in life. The voice with which Jesus spoke is similar to the voice with which his Church speaks, almost two thousand years later, in the encyclical letter *Pacem in Terris* of Pope John XXIII:

> "Since women are becoming ever more conscious of their human dignity, they will not tolerate being treated as mere material instruments, but demand rights befitting a human person, both in domestic and in public life." (no. 41)

There are many ways in which we can echo the voice of Jesus, and that of his Church, in proclaiming the dignity of both the male and female sexes, and of the Sacrament of Matrimony. Some ways which we might choose can become excessively dramatic, and draw unnecessary attention to the odd views of those who do not share the vision of Christianity and the Church's patriarchs in the Jewish tradition. For this reason, wise people are becoming less and less interested in trying to ban or demonstrate against harmful influences which only feed on publicity, and which can often be best neutralized if they are ignored.

Recognize women's dignity

But we can strive, in a positive fashion, for recognition of the dignity of the married state. This means not giving in to the pressures of those who see formal marriage in a sacramental way as unnecessary or worthy of scorn. It means, on the other hand, not going along with some Catholics who have the odd notion that marriage is only a consolation prize for those who are not celibate. In addition, we can work constructively for the recognition of the human and civil rights of women, and men, in society generally. As we do this, we must ask ourselves if we in our own Church community discriminate against lectors, leaders of community worship, or extraordinary ministers of the Eucharist who are women. And if the answer should be yes, then we will certainly have to get our own household in order, since it is the mandate of the Church to proclaim the dignity of the members of Christ's body, male and female.

Twenty-eighth Sunday of the Year

The first reading, from the Old Testament book of Wisdom, is another of many personifications utilized in the sapiential books, this time of Wisdom herself (Ws 7:7-11). The theme of the liturgy is carried out in the second reading, from the New Testament letter to the Hebrews (Heb 4:12-13) which also reflects some personification of the Word of God. In the narration of the Gospel according to Mark (Mk 10:17-30) we have an enumeration of the commandments and a reminder of their importance, coupled with a warning for those who would attend too much to earthly riches.

Love of wisdom

The readings of today's liturgy all point in the direction of reminding us what we should be about. We should pray to God for guidance and wisdom, and we should respond to his will by keeping his word and his laws. This we should do in the liturgy, of course, but in all other things as well.

The message is conveyed, first, in the poetic language of the wisdom literature from the Old Testament, several centuries before the time of Jesus. Even today, the Jewish people from whose culture those words come are lovers of wisdom and learning in the ways of the Lord. Every person who claims the name of Christian should imitate his or her spiritual ancestors in this love of God and his word.

But this does not mean that the word of God will always be soothing. As the letter to the Hebrews reminds us, it will sometimes be hard to receive, for it "penetrates and divides soul and spirit, joints and marrow." The word of God, like a two-edged sword, will cut cleanly and deeply. It will cut through false fronts and facades, through outward appearances, to reveal the truth, and often an unpleasant truth indeed.

Speaking the same language, Jesus in the Gospel account according to Mark recalls for his audience the commandments of the Law. The follower of the Lord must not kill, steal, participate in sexual immorality or be dishonest. Those who do such things—we know from other utterances in the New Testament—will have no place among the People of God unless they repent and sin no more. And even that, Jesus goes on record as saying, is really a bare minimum for his followers. Added to those basic moral observances, the Lord tells us, should be a concern for others who are less fortunate than we are, and who are therefore our responsibility in the world. This is a hard thing to grasp, if we are at the same time trying to grasp our own treasure or possessions.

Room for the poor?

A serious reading of the Scripture will make clear that Jesus does not mandate religious poverty for everyone as a norm. Nor does he hold in contempt those who would make reasonable provisions for their own lives and families. But he calls into question, at least, those who are preoccupied or excessively concerned with storing up treasure in the world. Such persons, it would seem clear, have little or no time or energy left to concern themselves with the word of God, and the ways in which that word of God would apply in everyday circumstances. Moreover, such individuals would have no room in their minds and hearts for the poor.

Self-deception is easy

It becomes all too easy to deceive ourselves in matters like these. Sometimes, we tend to imagine the goals of Christian life as impossible—as indeed they are without God's grace. "For man it is impossible," the Lord tells us, "but not for God. With God all things are possible." But we can make the mistake of seeing the Christian ideal as so far beyond our reach that it makes no sense to even look towards it. The other error we can make, certainly, is to assume in our favor—that we are already fulfilling the words and will of Jesus as thoroughly as possible, and therefore we need give no further thought to any of these things.

We will need, of course, to seek the wisdom of the Lord, and his life-giving word, which "judges the reflections and thoughts of the heart." We can do this, in part, by our attention to the Bible readings in our liturgy of the word, and their application in the preaching of the Church. We can do it, also, by paying particular heed to our bishops and clergy, with the Pope as their head, in the many statements they make concerning a just social and economic order. During the past century, we have had Popes, bishops and clergy who have been particularly forthright in matters of social and economic justice, and we can follow their teachings in the Catholic press, in adult-education courses, in parish or diocesan discussion groups and the other forms which the Church provides for us. We will not necessarily agree, one with another, on each and every aspect of application for these social statements within the Church. But we can hardly even have intelligent or creative disagreement or discussion without some study into the background of these matters. One thing we can do, at once, to make clear our concern for the word of God in the world is making the time and taking the opportunity to study the social and economic teachings of the Church, and how we might come to apply these in our own lives.

Twenty-ninth Sunday of the Year

The first reading from the Old Testament book attributed to the prophet Isaiah affords us once more the familiar image of the servant (Is 53:10-11), who shall save many by suffering. The image of the servant reaches its fulfillment in the New Testament in Jesus, as the second reading (Heb 4:14-16) points out. In the Gospel according to Mark (Mk 10:35-45), it is stressed that authority and priestly ministry in Jesus' kingdom must mean service and witness, not vainglory.

Broadened sense of vocation

Have you looked at the "vocation ads" lately? These are the notices one can see in Catholic magazines and newspapers, or in the lobbies of churches and schools—sometimes they have even appeared in the so-called "secular press" or on buses—attempting to interest young men and women in ministry in and for the Church as priests, members of religious orders, lay ministers or deacons. These notices are different from those of only a few years ago in many ways. One obvious difference is that their scope is wider. We now envision the permanent diaconate, restored in the wake of the Second Vatican Council, as a vital area of the service of our ordained clergy. We know that, according to the practice of the Roman Church, either celibate or married men may be ordained deacons or perform necessary and valuable services in and for the community in the name of the Lord. Also, we see that the Church actively seeks many lay members of the Christian family to be of service in ways consonant with their callings, talents and experiences. In addition to these ministries, of course, the Church continues to stress the more traditionally familiar ministries of priests and members of religious orders.

Ministry means service

But the difference in "vocation ads" is far more than a difference in scope, or in terms of who might be called to ministry and in which forms. The chief difference, it seems, is that vocation recruitment in the Church today is consciously stressing the ministry in all of its forms as a literal fulfillment of what the word "ministry" means: *service.* And, many times, the Church wants to point out, this service will often take on the dimension of suffering with and for the People of God.

Superficial image of ministry

What we observe and call attention to at the present time has always been true. However, it has not always been fully realized in the community of the Church. Many people tell us in their autobiographical statements that they were attracted to service as a priest, a religious brother or sister, at least in part by the nicely furnished rectories, the respect and deference shown to members of the community who were in holy orders or religious vows, the well-appointed convents, the social prestige in the Catholic community which no lay person could realistically aspire to, or the education provided in seminary, abbey or convent. Then, they tell us, such people were disillusioned. We need hardly engage, now, in a detailed analysis of whose fault this disillusionment was. It is, in a way, doubtless the fault of the total community of human beings that is the Church. But the Church, today, is making deliberate attempts to make clear how superficial and even false such images of ministry are.

The minister in the Church must never be separated from the experience of the people in the community, and the sufferings of the people. In fact, the ideal minister is one whose own personal service includes a type of suffering—not sought for its own sake, in a masochistic fashion, but part of the ministry—which is sign and salvation for the rest of the total community he or she serves.

Imitating Jesus essential

It is along these lines that the Church is stressing ministry today. Therefore, the emphasis on married ministers as deacons, extraordinary ministers of the eucharist, ministers of music, ministers of the Word of God in liturgy and religious education, and so on. Therefore, too, the emphasis—or re-emphasis—on poverty and simplicity of life-style for all who serve the Church, whether in religious vows, in holy orders, or in lay life. Nowadays, we are seeing bishops installed with simpler and humbler ceremonies and celebrations, prelates in the Church de-emphasizing impressive titles and regalia, and priests avoiding personal comforts which the majority of their parishioners cannot have. Such ministers are trying to imitate Jesus, who—as today's reading from the letter to the Hebrews would have it—is not unable to sympathize with the rest of us.

Because we are human, we think too much of rank and position. Our Gospel story for today reminds us that even the first followers of Jesus fell into this trap, and needed to be rescued by his words: "Anyone among you who aspires to greatness must serve the rest. . . . The Son of Man has not come to be served but to serve—to give his life in ransom for the many."

Thirtieth Sunday of the Year

The survival of the People of God in the Old Testament is brought out in terms of the "remnant of Israel" (Jr 31:7-9), brought together by the Lord and those who would serve him. The role of one who serves the Lord is spelled out again in the selection from the letter to the Hebrews (Heb 5:1-6); who serves humbly serves God and his people. In the Gospel selection, we see that one who seeks the aid of the Lord from his servant need only ask it and it will be given freely (Mk 10:46-52).

Last week our Scripture readings called us to an awareness of ministry in the Church as service. This week the Biblical texts of the liturgy do the same. We are reminded, once more, of the humanity of our ministers and of their human needs and obligations in the name and service of the Lord and his people in the Church.

Catholics may not always realize these notions concretely. For too long, we have tended to imprison our ministers in little cages that we construct from the anxieties and limitations of our own minds and hearts. We isolate our servants in the Church, so often, from everyday or "normal" life, in our prejudices and preconceived notions, in a mental and emotional fortress far stronger than the walls of any monastery.

We have tended, over the years, to criticize female religious who do not dress the way we think nuns should look; lay ministers in the Church who do not imitate the style of the ordained clergy, but instead live as they should, as normal lay members of the Church; priests who fail to conform to the stereotyped images of the clerical life-style we remember from the old Bing Crosby movies. We are appalled at any suggestion that these people are at all like ourselves. We are willing to take a few good strong drinks on occasion, but are often unusually critical of a priest or a member of a religious order who does the same. We are attached to creature comforts to some extent, but seem surprised if any of our ministers should exhibit this same human tendency. Those of us who are married accept a sexual relationship as part and parcel of our lives, but we often reject the suggestion that a minister of the Church might be married—for this reason we often discriminate against the married deacon and the married lay servant of the Church in all too many instances, and we who make up the grass-roots Catholic community insist on celibacy for the priest far more inflexibly than the hierarchy of the Church (which has insisted on this, throughout only the Western Rites, for less than half of the Church's history, admitting of exceptions).

Then, after isolating our priests, our deacons, our other ministers in the Church in the way that we have, we complain that they seem to be aloof, or too isolated from the common experiences of the rest of us. We should know by now that we can hardly hope to have it both ways. The only way we can have it is according to the profoundly human way described in the letter to the Hebrews: "Every high priest is taken from among men and made their representative before God, to offer gifts and sacrifices for sins. He is able to deal patiently with erring sinners, for he is himself beset by weakness and so must make sin offerings for himself as well as for the people. One does not take this honor on his own initiative, but only when called by God. . . ."

Ministers are human

In a word, if we would have a truly effective ministry in the Church, and one which fully and genuinely meets human needs among the People of God, then *we must allow our ministers to be human.* And if we complain that our ministers too often are surrounded with the trappings of pomp, luxury, pseudo-asceticism and isolation, we must ask ourselves: did they ask to be put in that box, or did we do it to them for the sake of our needs and anxieties?

If we can answer, as we probably can, that we are the imprisoners of our servants in the Church, then we alone can end the imprisonment. We can do this in various ways.

One thing we can do is to recognize our ministers as fully human, as individuals rather than functionaries, and as friends. This does not mean we disregard their function or position, or cease to respect it, in the Church, but we should not impersonalize our fellow Christians, who happen to be ministers, into mere cogs in a big ecclesiastical wheel. To use an example: the fact that someone in our community happens to be a priest, nun, or deacon, or otherwise a minister of the Church, does not except them from such common human experiences as frustration, loneliness, uncertainty, the "blues," or the need for human companionship, friendship and understanding.

Among Catholics in the Roman Church, particularly, we need to respect the authority of the Church not only in its upholding of the tradition of celibacy, but also in its celebration of ministry by married members of the Church—lay ministers, deacons, and those few priests who are married (e.g., in the Eastern Rites). Also, we can cooperate with the Church's efforts to expand ministry for members of the Church regardless of whether they are male or female.

All are ultimately ministers

Finally, we can stress the fact that all of us, each according to his or her own circumstances, is a minister to the extent that we are servants of the Lord and his people. In cooperation with our officially designated ministers, lay and ordained, we should all join in the service of taking the people and gathering them from the ends of the earth, "... with the blind and the lame in their midst, the mothers and those with child ..." in love and witness to the Lord.

The Feast of All Saints (November 1)

The first reading, from Revelation (7:2-4, 9-14) illustrates the universality of God's call to men and of the Church of Christ; in the second of the two readings attributed to John (1 Jn 3:1-3), this universality of God's invitation is celebrated as a great gift to mankind. The Gospel selection (Mt 5:1-12) points out the virtues which might otherwise escape human attention and which are necessary for sanctity.

The beat generation

About twenty years ago, there developed in the North Beach section of San Francisco—and eventually in other places as well —a phenomenon or movement that took, or had assigned to it, the name of "the beat generation." Various observers tried to assign some significance to that label. Some suggested that it meant the members of this group were "beat" or exhausted by the events of the immediate past in their lives—World War II, the beginnings of the Cold War, and "the Korean conflict." Others thought that those who were "beat" were "beat" in the sense that they were defeated. According to this viewpoint, they were beaten by a society which was too competitive for them, and they had lost out. Another view, which finds some support in the literature of the "beat" authors of the time— Ferlinghetti, Kerouac, Ginsberg and the others—is that "beat" had a very different meaning. According to this interpretation, "beat" was an abbreviation or shorthand term for "beatitude," and this generation or group was blessed.

A lot of Christians would be uncomfortable with or intolerant of that last interpretation. After all, weren't the so-called "beatniks" dirty and immoral? Didn't they ridicule the work ethic, patriotism, and commonly accepted morality? Didn't they partake of illicit sex and drugs? And weren't their beards and other symbols of "non-conformity" really a conformity unto itself?

Excesses and tourism

There were a lot of excesses, immaturities and irresponsibilities that one could see in the "beat generation" phenomenon two decades ago. But it would be a mistake to look only at the surface, as the Gray Line tourist buses did when they drove past the Co-Existence Bagel Shop in San Francisco, telling people through a loudspeaker to "look at all the beatniks, now!"

Looking deeper into the possibility that there might have been blessedness in the "beat generation," we do well to consider the light which Scripture can afford this question, in the readings for All Saints' Day from the Roman Lectionary. The reading from John's first letter, and the Gospel account according to Matthew, make it clear that a follower of Jesus will necessarily be a non-conformist in society, to at least a certain extent. This will mean to share the fate of Jesus, who was himself ignored and ostracized by the "Establishment" that held sway during the time of his earthly ministry in his public life. It will mean to be, as Christ and in Christ, prophetic. As John's epistle so well puts it: "The reason the world does not recognize us is that it never recognized the Son. Dearly beloved, we are God's children now; what we shall later be has not yet come to light. We know that when it comes to light we shall be like him, for we shall see him as he is."

Jesus' followers are non-conformists

Such words will be important for the person who, in following Jesus, defends the environment in a culture that is all too quick to destroy it, or who will see to the protection of human life itself, when even that is so frequently endangered in society. To say that our air and our waters are precious beyond common understanding is to be virtually ignored. To insist that every human life—in the nursing home, in the womb, in the ghetto of poverty—is valuable is to defy a utilitarian spirit that seems to have taken too firm a hold on our ethical atmosphere. To say that we must revere and defend the individual dignity of every person—whatever his or her race or religion or socio-economic level—is to fly in the face of a society where the average man too often thinks just like his television friend Archie Bunker. Moreover, anyone who is dedicated to a life of honesty and integrity in this time and place is not likely to find much support, when corruption and deceit are so often excused with expressions like "Everybody does it" and "let me get my share of the spoils!"

To stand up for and to practice the values of the Gospel will often mean to be just what the "beatitudes" describe: it will mean being poor in spirit, sorrowing while hungering and thirsting for holiness, all the while showing mercy and making peace, even when persecuted and insulted for the sake of the Lord. This is *real* non-conformity, and real blessedness. At the same time, it is conformity of the best sort: conformity to the person and mission and message of Jesus the Christ.

There is talk these days of a return to some elements of the "fifties" life-style. If that means dullness, or selective memory, in the manner of excessive "nostalgia," it can hardly be helpful. If it includes a generation, or several generations, whose individuality and introspection will lead to non-conformity in the name and in the spirit of Christ, it could be salutary . . . even saintly.

Thirty-first Sunday of the Year

The first reading, from the Old Testament book of Deuteronomy (Dt 6:2-6), reminds Israel of her obligations to the One God and his Law. The second passage, from the New Testament letter to the Hebrews, stresses the ancient notion of priesthood as fulfilled in Jesus the high priest of the New Covenant (Heb 7:23-28). The commandments of the Lord are summarized in two, in the Gospel account according to Mark (Mk 12:28-34).

There is only one God

If there is one theme running through today's Biblical lessons in the liturgy, it is this: there is no other; there is only one. There is no other God but the One God of Abraham, Isaac and Jacob, the God of the Chosen People of Israel. There is no priest really worthy of the name except the Son of God, Jesus the Christ. There is no law to be followed excepting the law of this one Lord and God, in the three Persons we know as the Father, the Son and the Holy Spirit.

The Law must be observed

This is the lesson of which the Israelites of old are reminded in today's passage from the Book of Deuteronomy in the Old Covenant. This book has its basis in the belief that the Law of the Lord must always be observed and obeyed. The Israelites did not always remember this or act accordingly, we know, and so it became necessary to remind them in oral tradition and in writing, in the Holy Scriptures of the Old Testament.

The same lesson, of course, is important for us. Like the People of God in the centuries before Jesus' earthly mission, we too forget, frequently, the one God who alone can claim our allegiance and obedience. We, like the Israelites of ancient times, are very often tempted to worship other gods: money, power, prestige, human respect, pride and prejudice. Or, again like the Hebrews of old, we like to "hedge our bets," serving God in theory while at the same time attempting to serve as well one of the false gods we tend to embrace at once. We cannot do this, the Bible reminds us time and time again. We can serve only the one God, and the one God alone—or else we serve God not at all.

Priesthood

The People of Israel realized the importance of being connected to God by a mediator, or priest. In the New Covenant, this image of priesthood is fulfilled beyond all expectation in the person and the priesthood of the mediator who is the Christ, the anointed Messiah, our Lord Jesus. Anyone whom we in the Church call by the name of priest is not a priest in his own right or by his own power, but only is a priest in so far as he corresponds and conforms to the priestly mission of Jesus, and derives his priestly authority from Jesus by submitting to his divine will as exercised through the Apostles and their successors to whose custody Jesus' priesthood in the world is entrusted.

All of this sounds as though it is difficult to be a follower of Jesus in any capacity, let alone that of ordained priesthood in the Church. Indeed it is difficult. It is more than difficult to be a follower and representative of the One God who sends the Son, Jesus, as high priest. At the same time, we are consoled by Jesus' priestly presence in the Sacraments of the Church, most especially the sacrificial banquet of the Eucharistic Liturgy, or the Mass.

This means that if we would be truly connected to or in

harmony with the one God whom we would serve, we must be so connected by means of and in light of the Sacraments of the Church, and the Church as sacramental society. Despite whatever urges toward autonomy might loom large in our individual egos and personalities, we cannot be "loners" or "go it alone." Instead, we necessarily come together, in the name of the Lord, to partake of his presence in the Service of the Word and the Service of the Eucharist.

Responsibility

This very fact in itself places even an increased responsibility upon the People of God in the New Covenant, and upon priests ordained in the service of the People of God most especially. Most of us have probably been taught that the Mass and the other Sacraments retain their efficacy, keep us connected to the Persons of the Trinity in that life which we call sacramental grace, even when the rites are rushed through in a fashion which is slovenly and even irreverent. While that might be quite true in terms of the minimal assurances of the law of the Church and of the bare necessities of sacramental theology, it is hardly sufficient for the life we must live if we are to follow the one God and be united to the deity through the high priest, Jesus.

We must, therefore, continue to be attentive to the liturgy of the Church, in both the Service of the Word and the Liturgy of the Eucharist, and take care to see to ways in which we can render its celebration more fitting and more meaningful for each of us as members of the priestly People of God over which Jesus the high priest presides in a special capacity. And as we come towards the end of one liturgical year, and begin preparing for another, according to the calendar of the Church, this is an especially good time to take stock of our progress in this.

Thirty-second Sunday of the Year

The first reading, from the first of the Old Testament books of Kings (1 K 17:10-16), is one among many prophetic insistences on God's providence for those who will follow his way. In the second reading, from the New Testament letter to the Hebrews (Heb 9:24-28), continues a theme exposed in last week's liturgy of the Word: Christ is the eternal high priest. In the Gospel according to Mark (Mk 12:38-44), Jesus is seen cautioning people against the pride of the ostentatious ones, and urging instead the imitation of the poor widow.

A familiar story

Almost everyone is familiar with the story told in the Gospel today. We are so familiar with it, perhaps, that we are in danger of failing to pay attention to it. As with so many other stories from the Bible, there is a temptation to say, "Oh, yes, we've heard that one already," and then tune the channel-selector of our minds to what appears a more intriguing program.

In the case of today's Gospel account, perhaps one reason we are quick to turn away is that we don't like the message behind the story. We are uncomfortable, often, with the implications of this narrative, and we would rather concentrate on something more soothing or less challenging.

It is tough

As the world economic picture is less than encouraging, at

best, our own personal economic situation is by no means cause for rejoicing, either. As a result, we are not likely to listen with rapt attention to a Gospel which instructs us more and more in the direction of generosity.

Anyone who goes to buy bread or milk or vegetables in our supermarkets, anyone who has to pay for fuel for the family car, or public transit fares for commuting, anyone who has to pay repairmen's fees, rent, tuition or taxes, is not going to be enthusiastic about an appeal for generosity. We have it pretty rough ourselves, we feel. And, in fact, we are right. It is tough.

The problem is, though, that it is far tougher for many others in the world, especially in whole countries and even entire continents where there is widespread poverty or famine. Even in our own country, there are those who, through no fault of their own, are destitute. Despite whatever we may assume about government and private charity, these people are not provided for adequately.

What can we do?

All right—what can be done by us? What can be done by those many of us who are, ourselves, victims of an economic situation which is full of uncertainty and injustice? The answer, whether we are anxious to hear it or not, lies in the story of the Gospel today. We are not called upon by the Lord to give out of our excess or surplus wealth, for indeed, we have none. On the contrary, we are asked to give when we can, and what we can, out of what we need—or feel we need—for ourselves. This means the asking of some hard questions on the part of each and every one of us:

Do I really need a new coat this year? Can I cut down on smoking or drinking? Might I seek and enjoy less expensive forms of entertainment? Can I do with less expensive food on the table? And this last question applies to the rectory table as surely as it does to any other—perhaps more so.

In most cases, the answers to the questions will point in this direction: of course it will require even further sacrifice than we are already making in a time of austerity, but this austerity can take place not only out of necessity but also out of love of the Lord. And the sacrifice can be made for the sake of contributing what we can, out of our hard-earned salaries as office worker or policeman or clergyman or professional or factory worker, to the poor of the world.

The amount may be small

The amount of any individual contribution along these lines might not be able to be much in itself, surely. It might equal only the price of a drink, or a pack of cigarettes or a pouch of tobacco or box of cigars. It might be equivalent to only the admission to a movie or ball game or play. It could be no more than the difference between a small and a large soft drink or between a small and a large order of french fries at the local hamburger palace. And it will come from resources, or monies, which are truly and legitimately our own, which we have every right to. It will not be from surplus wealth, or from "left-over" funds.

Jesus, in the story given us in the Gospel today, does not ask us to throw in the direction of the poor those things we do not want, or feel we can easily get along without. He asks pretty much the opposite: he asks us to sacrifice from among the things we feel we *should* have, and are entitled to. This was what the widow did with her meager funds. This is the model provided for us.

Thirty-third Sunday of the Year

The series for today's Service of the Word opens with a reading from the prophetic book of Daniel (Dn 12, 1-3), envisioning the day of the Lord that will come. Jesus, in the Gospel selection according to Mark (Mk 13:24-32), is depicted as predicting a similar day—some have interpreted this as a figurative description of the Fall of Jerusalem, others the Second Coming of Jesus. The second reading (Heb 10:11-14, 18) stresses the day-to-day nature of ministry in priesthood.

The readings for today are ominous to us. The first, from the Old Testament, speaks of what appears a destructive and frightening day. The images presented in the Gospel are not much more encouraging or reassuring. We should not be distressed, though, at these things. Rather, we should remember what scholars of the Bible have told us for years: these are images in oral tradition—and eventually in the written Word of God in the Old and New Testaments—intended to convey a mood of events to come which will end the "old order." Moreover, the scholars tell us, it is not utterly certain which events are being imagined in these utterances. Some say the destruction of Jerusalem and the Temple there; others say the dispersion of the Jews after Jerusalem's fall; still others believe Jesus' imagery refers to his own Second Coming in final triumph and glory, when the world as we know it will come to a final consummation.

The "end of the world"

Some of the early followers of Jesus believed this "end of

the world" would be imminent. They tended to view their so-
journ in the world as being of such a fleeting nature that they
saw little point in adjusting the circumstances of their presence
here. As a result, those who were married were advised to remain married, but those who were single were advised not to
marry. Likewise, the early Christians tended to tolerate some
injustices, like slavery, rather than press for their reform, since
they believed time was short indeed.

Exaggeration yields panic

There have been a number of times, in history, when people
believed the "end of the world" to be imminent. Some individuals
felt this when the year of our Lord 1000 was coming. Others
felt that the world would end in 1960, because some people had
misinterpreted and exaggerated certain private revelations. And
there have been other examples throughout history when people
felt sure they knew that the world was coming to an "end."
In some of these cases, the reaction was fright or panic. In
some others, it may have been anxious anticipation.

We are all reminded by the Scriptures and by the teaching
Church that no one of us, not even all of us together, can predict the Second Coming of Jesus. We can prepare for his final
triumph, and the fulfillment of history—what we commonly call
the world's coming to its "end" or goal—only in the way we
see described so admirably in the Epistle to the Hebrews, the
second reading for today's liturgy: day by day ministry, "and
offering again and again . . . sacrifices."

This reading points out, rightly, that no human sacrifice
in itself can take away sin and its effects. Only the one sacrifice
offered by Jesus can do that. However, as members of Jesus'
body the Church we are able to unite our own lives and sacrifices with his, sacramentally. We can participate in the one
offering he has made as our high priest.

Day by day

We cannot do this in a way that is anxious or arrogant.

We cannot do it with the certainty that things will end at this time or in that manner. We members of Christ in the Church can do it in only the way described to us by this reading: day by day ministry—a ministry which is worth while not for the other priests of the world, but for the one priest, Jesus, in whose priesthood and ministry all members of the body of Christ share.

This will not be at all dramatic. It hardly measures up to the imagery of "the Son of Man coming in the clouds with great power and glory" or even "a time unsurpassed in distress." But it will be a way of contributing to the final glory which will be that of the Son of Man and savior of mankind, Jesus.

A good time to reflect

We are approaching the end of one liturgical year and the beginning of another one. This is as good a time as any to reflect on the year ending and the one about to commence. How do we participate in the priesthood of Jesus, the one true priest? How do we unite our daily sufferings with his, for the salvation of the world? How do we serve others in the *body* of Christ and in the *name* of Christ? If our answers to these questions, asked honestly, leave us unsatisfied, then we are in a position to re-evaluate and re-align our lives as members of that worshipping community of ministry which is the Church. We can take stock of our participation in the liturgy, and especially in that sort of Christian life which should radiate from the liturgy in faith, hope and fraternal love.

Thirty-fourth or Last Sunday of the Year—Christ The King

The liturgy begins once more with a reading from the book of Daniel (Dn 7:13-14). This image of Son of Man, which Jesus fulfills, is brought out as well in the selection from the Apocalypse, or Book of Revelation (Rv 1:5-8). The Gospel hastens to point out, in the narrative according to John, the unworldly nature of the kingship of Jesus (Jn 18:33-37).

The richness of language fails

Human language is beautiful and rich, in so many instances. The great writers of the ages, the celebrated poets, the playwrights, all have given us a host of memorable expressions. Moreover, they are still doing it. Language—whether in writing or in oral communication—is a beautiful gift from God, whereby we can express a multitude of realities, relationships and reactions. Sometimes, though, for all its majesty and power in communication, language can let us down. With all our attempts at vivid clarity and impeccable logic or precise definition, language can somehow fail to convey exactly what it is that we wish to speak about, describe or communicate.

In particular, language lets us down when we describe— or *attempt* to describe—the Lord and man's relationship to him. This should not surprise us too much, however. After all, has this not been the experience of the great philosophers and theologians? Augustine found it so, and after him Thomas Aquinas, who could only define what God was *not*, since God does not admit of the limits of direct definition. Other Christian writers and thinking people, despite their intelligence, have found the same problem. And theology, we are all aware, is not so much a science or definition of God as it is a study of a Word that he reveals to us, rather than a cataloguing of words we impose on God.

Concrete terms

The people who gave us the oral traditions that were set down in the Bible had an advantage over us, besides the obvious fact of divine inspiration. That advantage, we are told, was in the fact that these individuals tended to express themselves not in philosophical terms or intellectual categories, but rather in concrete existential images. We are forever in the debt of those who produced the kind of culture wherein the Lord could be seen as a gentle shepherd, or the people of the Covenant as his sheep.

But sometimes even this beautiful language, as found in the Scriptures, is in danger of missing the mark, by even a wide margin, if we are not careful in our use of it or our response to it. A prime example is the imagery of today's Biblical readings. Passages such as these have given rise to a host of hymns, poems, sermons, writings, and ideas about Jesus, or the Persons of the Trinity together, as seated on a throne, or being crowned, after the fashion of earthly rulers of old. In one sense, we are able to appreciate the symbols involved: Jesus is Lord, meaning he has ultimate dominion and power, much as a king would have in an absolute monarchy. Moreover, our God would be worshipped and adored, even far beyond whatever homage would be due any temporal ruler. But beyond that point, we may become confused.

We may, in fact, fall into the same trap as those described in today's Gospel, according to John, who were ready to mistake Jesus' kingdom as being of the world. We know that the disciples of Jesus, even, were in danger of this misinterpretation, and that Our Lord frequently reminded them of the contrary.

A different kingdom

We may remember that Jesus' kingdom is truly of another order, and of a life which is supernatural and not merely confined to the here-and-now. But we might not apply all of the meaning of this to ourselves. We who make up the Church, or the People of God in the New Covenant, are ever in danger of piling up for ourselves and for our own institutions the very things that an earthly king would go after: prestige, power, abundant material riches, all in ways which are excessive, unneccesary, and perpetuating injustice and alienation between human beings in the world. While it can be argued that some material good, some prestige may be necessary at times for the mission of the Church, there is always a danger associated with such things. We should always be on the lookout, and always ready to ask ourselves some hard questions: Is this or that good— in terms of power or worldly goods—really fitting and needed for the loving ministry of Jesus in the world, and in particular for my share, or our share, in that ministry? Am I, or are we, going after power and prestige for our own sake, our *own* glorification? The answers, of course, will not be identical in each and every situation, nor should we expect them to be. But we must ask the questions, reply to them as honestly as we can, and act accordingly. For if we partake in any way of the kingdom of Christ, our whole purpose should be simply to testify to the truth.